HOLINESS

THEMES
from
ST THÉRÈSE OF LISIEUX

ALOYSIUS REGO OCD

With a Foreword by James McCaffrey OCD

First published 2009 by:

TERESIAN PRESS
Carmelite Priory
Boars Hill
Oxford OX1 5HB
priory@carmelite.org.uk

Copyright © Aloysius Rego, OCD 2009

ISBN 978-0-947916-10-7

A catalogue record for this book is available from the British Library.

Quotations from the writings of St Thérèse of Lisieux
© Washington Province of Discalced Carmelites ICS Publications
2131 Lincoln Road, N.E. Washington, DC 20002-1199 U.S.A.
www.icspublications.org

Cover photograph © Office Central de Lisieux
It depicts Thérèse as Joan of Arc in prison
in her play *Joan of Arc Accomplishing Her Mission*,
performed in the Carmel of Lisieux on January 21, 1895.

Cover design by Bill Bolger

Typeset and printed by Joshua Horgan, Oxford

Therefore all in the Church...are called to holiness

(Lumen Gentium 39)

For my family:

> *my father, a man of prayer*
>> *my mother, a woman of selfless giving*
>>> *my siblings, who help to shape and form me*

With gratitude for your inspiration, love and sacrifices

TABLE OF CONTENTS

FOREWORD

This is a book of substance, quality and depth. It is to be read and pondered slowly and prayerfully. True to its title, *Holiness For All*, it reaffirms the teaching of Vatican II on the universal call to holiness. It offers us deep insights into many of the major themes in the writings of St Thérèse, as seen through the eyes of an author captivated by her deep spirituality – something he is eager to share with others.

The book requires no previous knowledge of the writings of Thérèse, only an openness to the impact of the saint's teachings. Many books have been written about Thérèse. But this is one that allows the saint to speak for herself, unimpeded, in her own inspired words and images. Writing in a clear, simple and crisp style, the author shows that her spirituality is accessible and intelligible to all.

This book is not written primarily for scholars – although the specialist will find a deep pool of inspiration in these pages, with frequent quotations from Thérèse and ample cross-references to facilitate further research. But first and foremost, it is an inestimable gift to all who wish to reflect on her teachings quietly and prayerfully, allowing her message to take root in a heart open to be led by Thérèse into her secret of holiness.

A brief Prologue outlines the main themes explored in the book: the Scriptures, the Little Way, Prayer, the Merciful Love of God, and Truth; as well as the context of the saint's family and an overview of her writings. Other significant themes like Mary, the Eucharist, and Fraternal Love are also touched upon, and the author assures us that he is currently working on other themes; we eagerly await his further illuminating insights. With consummate skill, he is at pains to stress and articulate for us the gradual development and growth in Thérèse's ever-deepening understanding of her own teachings. She had to grope her way and struggle, slowly and painfully, to the full flowering of her spirituality.

To savour this book is to embark on a marvellous voyage of discovery from the first stirrings of God's grace in the soul of Thérèse as she searches to surrender herself unreservedly, in her own unique way, to the boundless mercy of God – through the darkness of her 'night of faith' to her final transformation in love. It is reassuring to know that we travel in the company of this most recent Doctor of the Church and one who has rightly been called by Pope Pius X 'the greatest saint of modern times'.

James McCaffrey, OCD

ABBREVIATIONS

The Major Works

SS   *Story of a Soul: The Autobiography of Saint Thérèse of Lisieux*, tr. John Clarke, OCD, Washington, DC: ICS Publications, 1996.

GC I   *Saint Thérèse of Lisieux: General Correspondence, Volume I (1877-1890)*, tr. John Clarke, OCD, Washington, DC: ICS Publications, 1982.

GC II   *Saint Thérèse of Lisieux: General Correspondence, Volume II (1890-1897)*, tr. John Clarke, OCD, Washington, DC: ICS Publications, 1988.

LT   Letters of Thérèse of Lisieux: in GC I & GC II.

LC   *St. Thérèse of Lisieux: Her Last Conversations*, tr. John Clarke, OCD, Washington, DC: ICS Publications, 1977.

Memoirs and Testimonies

MSST   Sister Geneviève of the Holy Face (Céline Martin), *My Sister St. Thérèse*, tr. The Carmelite Sisters of New York, Rockford, IL: Tan Books & Publishers, 1997.

Test   Christopher O'Mahony (ed. & tr.), *St Thérèse of Lisieux by Those who Knew Her: Testimonies from the Process of Beatification*, Dublin: Veritas Publications, 1975.

PROLOGUE

The year 1997 marked the centenary of the death of Thérèse of Lisieux, one of the most popular and best-loved saints of the Catholic Church in the early and mid twentieth century. To mark this event, the Discalced Carmelite Order engaged in a concerted effort to revive interest in her, by making her life and doctrine more widely accessible through retreats and public lectures.

It was during this time that I was invited by the superior of the Discalced friars in Australia to be involved in the project of disseminating Thérèse's doctrine and spirituality. The chapters of this book contain, in a slightly modified form, the talks that I gave in retreats and public events.

My main aim in these lectures was rather modest. It was not to treat the themes exhaustively, or in a highly academic manner, but simply to help my audience engage with Thérèse's writings by opening these up to them. To this end I have, as much as possible, put together the texts in such a way as to enable the audience to hear Thérèse speak for herself. My hope was that, at the conclusion of the lectures, my listeners would be enthused and encouraged to read for themselves the writings of this youngest and most recent Doctor of the Church.

I did not attempt to apply her message directly to the situation of my audience, but left this to each particular listener to do so for himself or herself. Rather, through introducing the texts, I hope to show that the deceptive simplicity of Thérèse's doctrine contains a wealth of spiritual wisdom from which everyone can profit in his or her own way and circumstances. Each person has a unique and individual relationship with God. And this also means a personal itinerary by which each of us journeys to God. So, I do believe that the saints are not given to us solely for our imitation: first and foremost, they are there for our *inspiration*. In short, there will be some elements in the spirituality of the saints that we will find attractive and helpful, and others that we do not fully agree with or find applicable to our own experience and situation.

While some knowledge of Thérèse's life is essential, I have not retold her life-story in detail, as there are many biographies readily available. Instead, I have included a chapter introducing the significant and influential figures in Thérèse's life, as well as the more important events that marked her. My main concern, in *Holiness For All*, is with breaking open some of the major themes that emerge in the saint's writings. These themes are: the Scriptures, the Little Way, Prayer, God, and Truth. Of course, they are by no means the only ones in the works of Thérèse, and I am currently working on others.

The book is arranged as follows:

Chapter One, as mentioned, takes the place of a biography by exploring briefly some of the **significant relationships and events** in Thérèse's life. This chapter will enable those who are not very familiar with these facts to acquire enough information to engage with the chapters that follow.

Chapter Two looks at the major **writings** of Thérèse. It explores the nature and content of each of the works, their origin, and how they came to the attention of the public.

Chapter Three examines the place of the **Scriptures** in Thérèse's life and how she used the word of God in her life and spiritual journey.

Chapter Four explores Thérèse's spirituality of the **Little Way**. It investigates the dynamics by which she came to discover her own spirituality, and considers the dispositions which, with God's grace, we need to cultivate in order to live this 'little way'.

Chapter Five reflects on the whole area of **prayer** in the life and spirituality of Thérèse. It explores such questions as: Where did Thérèse learn to pray? For whom did she pray? How did she understand the nature of prayer? What were some of the difficulties she encountered in prayer, and how did she manage them?

Chapter Six considers Thérèse's understanding of God as **Merciful Love**. This also covers the issue of how she dealt with the conundrum of God's mercy versus God's justice.

Chapter Seven examines the place of **truth** in the life and spirituality of Thérèse. Truth is an important Theresian virtue, and it influences many aspects of her spirituality.

Although much of the material is the result of my personal study of Thérèse's works, I have been helped and inspired by my reading of various works on her. Those which have influenced me most are those of Hans Urs von Balthasar,[1] Conrad De Meester,[2] and François Jamart.[3]

This book is the result of the encouragement I received from many members of my audience at retreats and other gatherings. To them I express my thanks and gratitude for allowing me to share with them my love for Thérèse and her spirituality.

I also wish to acknowledge my heartfelt gratitude and thanks to the following:

– my parents (George and Celine) who, without any intellectual knowledge of Thérèse, were the first to model for me the living of her Little Way;

– Sr Marie Thérèse Long, OSB for her valuable comments and suggestions during the preparation of this work;

– Fr James McCaffrey, OCD for readily accepting to write the Foreword and for being such an excellent Editor, together with Joanne Mosley who has shown such great dedication in working on my book;

– Sheila Cooper and Geraldine Long for their persistence and prayers in encouraging me to put these talks into print.

Chapter One

SIGNIFICANT RELATIONSHIPS AND EVENTS

We exist, and are shaped, within a web of relationships. Of course, the first such 'web' we encounter is the one into which we are born: the family. For many of us, if not all, the family of origin is arguably the most powerful influence in our life, shaping us for good or ill. So, it is important to begin by introducing some of the main figures who constituted the web of relationships that formed Thérèse; these characters were mainly, but not exclusively, members of her family. We will also take a brief look at Thérèse's personality, and present some of the significant events in her life which had a bearing on her spiritual growth.

I. Significant Relationships

1. Thérèse's Parents

Thérèse was born into a very close-knit, devout, middle-class Catholic family in Alençon, Normandy on January 2, 1873. She was the youngest of nine children, consisting of seven girls and two boys. Only five girls survived into adulthood; the other two girls and both boys died young.

*

Her father, **Louis Martin**, married late in life – at the age of 35 – after failing to gain acceptance into the monastery of the Great St Bernard when he was 22. He was a devout and prayerful man, with a contemplative and solitary temperament, who loved fishing. Thérèse recalls, in *Story of a Soul*, that she had only to look at her father at prayer to see how the saints pray (cf. SS, p. 43). By trade, Louis was a reasonably successful jeweller and watchmaker. Thérèse had a particularly close relationship with her father and a deep love for him.

In *Story of a Soul*, Thérèse confesses: 'I wasn't even able to think of Papa *dying* without trembling' (SS, pp. 47-8). She narrates the following incident, which reveals her deep attachment to her father:

> Once he had climbed to the top of a ladder and as I was standing directly below, he cried out: 'Move away, little one, if I fall, I'll crush you!' When I heard this, I experienced an interior revulsion and instead of moving away I clung to the ladder, thinking: 'At least, if Papa falls, I'll not have the grief of seeing him die; I'll die with him!' (SS, p. 48)

This deep attachment between father and daughter was mutual and reciprocated. Thérèse used to refer to Louis as 'my king', and he called her 'my little queen'; it is quite evident that she idolised and adored her father. Her relationship with him most certainly had a significant influence on how she saw and related to God.

Thérèse often refers to her father as a 'saint'. In one of her letters to him soon after entering Carmel, she writes: 'When I think of you, dear little Father, I naturally think of God, for it seems to me that it is impossible to see anyone more holy than you on the earth' (LT 58). Louis, then, had a profound formative influence on Thérèse's life and spiritual development.

Louis was from Bordeaux but had settled in Alençon, where he met and married Thérèse's mother, Zélie Guérin.

*

Zélie Guérin was from near Alençon, a town famous for its lace-making industry. Like Louis, she was a failed applicant to the religious life; she herself became a competent lace-maker with her own successful business. Zélie, too, married rather late in life – at the age of 27 – and was 42 when Thérèse, her last child, was born. Like her husband, Zélie was a person of deep faith. She was also a hard worker and the more practical of the two.

Soon after Thérèse's birth, Zélie, who was too ill to suckle the baby, had to find a wet-nurse for her child. Already, the first signs of breast cancer – which eventually led to Zélie's death – were manifesting themselves. Hence, Thérèse spent the crucial first year of her life with Rose Taillé at Semallé – about six miles from Alençon.

Even though Thérèse did not have much time with her mother – she was only four when Zélie died – she was nevertheless emotionally close to her. Zélie's death, then, was a great blow to the child and a cause of deep sadness and trauma, as we will see later.

The following incident, recounted in Zélie's letters and quoted by Thérèse, speaks of the emotional bond between them:

> The little one has just placed her hand on my face and kissed me. This poor little thing doesn't want

to leave me; she's continually at my side. She likes going into the garden, but when I'm not there she won't stay but cries till they bring her to me... Little Thérèse asked me the other day if she would go to Heaven. I told her 'Yes' if she were good. She answered: 'Yes, but if I'm not good, I'll go to hell. But I know what I will do. I will fly to you in Heaven, and what will God be able to do to take me away? You will be holding me so tightly in your arms!' I could see in her eyes that she was really convinced that God could do nothing to her if she were in her mother's arms. (SS, p. 18)

Little Thérèse felt so secure and safe in her mother's arms that she really believed God was powerless to touch her there. So it is not surprising that, with her mother's death, she says her 'happy disposition completely changed' (SS, p. 34).

A few months after Zélie's death, Louis moved with his family of five daughters to Lisieux – the town that would come to be associated with the future saint – in order to be close to his wife's family, the Guérins.

2. Thérèse's Sisters

All the surviving sisters became nuns. Four of them, Marie, Pauline, Céline and Thérèse, entered the Carmel of Lisieux. Léonie joined the Visitation Order, founded by St Jeanne de Chantal, a close friend of St François de Sales. Thérèse was close to all her sisters.

*

Pauline, the second-eldest child in the family, was the sibling who was most influential in Thérèse's growth and development. In *Story of a Soul*, Thérèse confesses that as a child – even before her mother's death – Pauline was her favourite sister, the one to whom she felt most drawn. She writes:

I was very proud of my two sisters [Marie and Pauline], but the one who was my *ideal* from childhood was Pauline. When I was beginning to talk, Mama would ask me: 'What are you thinking about?' and I would answer invariably: 'Pauline!' Another time, I was moving my little finger over the windowpanes and I said: 'I'm writing Pauline!' (SS, p. 20)

It is not surprising, then, that Thérèse adopted Pauline as her second mother after Zélie's death. Pauline was Thérèse's ideal and model, the one who inspired her and whom she emulated. This is what she says:

I had often heard it said that surely Pauline would become a *religious*, and without knowing too much about what it meant I thought: '*I* too *will be a religious.*' This is one of my first memories and I haven't changed my resolution since then! It was through you, dear Mother [Pauline], that Jesus chose to espouse me to Himself. You were not with me then, but already a bond was formed between our souls. You were my *ideal*; I wanted to be like you, and it was your example that drew me toward the Spouse of Virgins at the age of two. (SS, p. 20)

Here it is evident how deeply formative was the influence of Pauline on the young Thérèse. Pauline was her 'second mother', and Thérèse was strongly attached to her. Pauline was the first of the Martin sisters to join the Lisieux Carmel – in 1882, when Thérèse was only nine. The separation was to have a drastic effect on the child's life and well-being.

The psychological blow suffered by Thérèse is undeniable and understandable – for, although still a child, she had already suffered three *significant* separations: the first, at six weeks old, from her mother Zélie; the second, at one year of age, from Rose Taillé, her wet-nurse; and the third, at the age of four, from her mother when Zélie died. Now, at the age of nine, Thérèse was losing Pauline, whom she had clung to as her 'second mother'. It is not surprising that about five months after Pauline's entry into the convent, Thérèse became seriously ill with a kind of nervous breakdown and delirium. This illness, which lasted around six weeks, was cured by a miraculous smile of the Blessed Virgin which she perceived on the statue of Mary in her room. In Carmel, Pauline was given the name 'Agnes of Jesus'.

*

With Pauline's entry into Carmel, **Marie**, the eldest child and Thérèse's godmother, assumed the duty of Thérèse's principal carer. She played an important role in the child's physical, emotional, psychological and spiritual growth. She was responsible for preparing Thérèse for her First Communion and Confirmation, and in many ways she was Thérèse's confidante and spiritual guide. Thérèse reports that she lived in complete obedience to Marie's directions, especially during her struggle with scrupulosity.[1]

With the departure of Marie to the Lisieux Carmel in 1886, Thérèse, now 13, was to suffer yet another major emotional and psychological blow. She expresses her relationship with Marie at this time as follows: she was 'the only support of my soul. It was Marie who guided, consoled, and aided me in the practice of virtue; she was my sole oracle... Marie knew, then, everything that went on in my soul, and she knew my desires for Carmel. I loved her so much I couldn't live without her' (SS, p. 88). It is not surprising, then, that when she learnt of Marie's impending departure for Carmel, Thérèse expressed her great disappointment with life: 'I resolved to take no pleasure out of earth's attractions' (SS, p. 90). In the convent, Marie was given the name 'Marie of the Sacred Heart'.

*

Léonie was, so to speak, the 'black sheep' of the Martin family. She was the rebel of the household and something of an embarrassment and worry to the family. Unlike her sisters, she did not always toe the party line or meet the expectations of her parents. In addition she was, both physically and intellectually, less gifted than her sisters. It seems that she was a problem child: emotionally disturbed and with learning difficulties. In *Story of a Soul*, Thérèse does not mention her as often as she does her other sisters; and Léonie does not appear to be as formative an influence on Thérèse. Regarding her relationship with Léonie, Thérèse acknowledges:

> Dear little Léonie held a warm place in my heart. She was very fond of me and in the evenings when the family took a walk she used to take care of me. I still seem to hear those beautiful lullabies she used to sing to me to get me to sleep. She was always trying to find ways of pleasing me, and I would be sorry if I caused her any trouble. (SS, pp. 20-1; cf. p. 64)

Thérèse tells us that on a visit to Alençon with her father, Céline and herself, Léonie rather impetuously joined

23

the Poor Clares but did not remain long with them (cf. SS, p. 92). Later, Léonie made two more unsuccessful attempts to try out her vocation in the religious life, with the Visitation Sisters. Finally, after Thérèse's death, she tried again and this time persevered, dying in the odour of sanctity at the Visitation convent in Caen. It is said that Léonie truly embraced and lived out Thérèse's spirituality of the Little Way.

*

Céline was almost four years older than Thérèse, yet she was her constant childhood companion (cf. SS, p. 21). They were very close and intimate. Thérèse quotes from one of Zélie's letters to illustrate this: 'Céline and Thérèse are inseparable and it's impossible to see two children love each other so much' (SS, p. 26). Thérèse also confesses: 'I remember that I really wasn't able to be without Céline. I'd sooner leave the table without taking my dessert than not to follow her as soon as she got up' (SS, p. 26).

As for her mature relationship with Céline, she describes it as 'the same soul giving us life' (SS, p. 106). This relationship was so close, said Thérèse, that 'if I had to recount everything I would never come to an end' (SS, p. 55). And Céline testified to the tribunal for the beatification of Thérèse: 'During our childhood days Thérèse and I were inseparable' (MSST, p. 109). This closeness and intimacy remained until Thérèse's death.

Thérèse's deep love for Céline is revealed in her great desire that Céline join her in Carmel. Thérèse could not endure the thought that Céline would get married or somehow not belong to Jesus in an *exclusive* way. Just as belonging *solely* to Jesus was Thérèse's cherished desire, so she ardently desired this gift for Céline whom she loved deeply. In *Story of a Soul*, she recalls her anguish at the possibility that Céline would marry and not be a 'spouse of Jesus':

> the most intimate of my desires, the greatest of them all, which I thought would never be realised, was my dear Céline's entrance into the same Carmel as ours. This *dream* appeared to be improbable: to live under the same roof, to share the joys and pains of the companion of my childhood; I had made my sacrifice complete by confiding to Jesus my dear sister's future, resolved to see her leave for the other side of the world if necessary. The only thing I couldn't accept was her not being the spouse of Jesus, for since I loved her as much as I loved myself it was impossible for me to see her give her heart to a mortal being. (SS, p. 176)

Céline was the last of the four Martin girls to join the Lisieux convent. She nursed her father, Louis, until his death in 1894, and two months later entered Carmel. There, she was given the name 'Geneviève of the Holy Face'.

3. The Prioress

There is another significant character in Thérèse's life, though not a member of her family. **Mother Marie de Gonzague**, who was almost 40 years older than Thérèse, was prioress at the Lisieux convent for all but three years of Thérèse's religious life. In *Story of a Soul*, if we read between the lines, Marie de Gonzague comes across as a formidable and dark character who was psychologically a little erratic. Yet, undoubtedly, she possessed some attractive qualities. She must have been a charismatic person with good leadership qualities for the nuns to keep re-electing her as their prioress. Many of the younger ones – including Thérèse – seemed to have been greatly attracted to her.[2] Marie de Gonzague was one of the first persons to learn of Thérèse's desire to be a Carmelite nun, and also one of the few, apart from Pauline (cf. SS, p. 106), to encourage her in her vocation. In *Story of a Soul*, addressing Mother Marie, Thérèse says:

> Many of the Sisters think that you spoiled me, that since my entrance into the holy ark, I have received from you nothing but caresses and compliments. Nevertheless it was not so. You will see, dear Mother, in the copybook containing my childhood memories [Manuscript A], what I think of the *strong* and maternal education I received from you. From the bottom of my heart I want to thank you for not sparing me. Jesus knew very well that His little flower stood in need of the living waters of humiliation, for she was too weak to take root without this kind of help, and it was through you, dear Mother, that this blessing was given to me. (SS, p. 206)

And, recounting her relationship with Mother Marie to Pauline, she writes:

> our Mother Prioress, frequently ill, had little time to spend with me. I know that she loved me very much and said everything good about me that was possible, nevertheless, God permitted that she was VERY SEVERE *without her even being aware of it*. I was unable to meet her without having to kiss the floor [a custom when a religious was corrected for a fault],

and it was the same thing on those rare occasions when she gave me spiritual direction. (SS, p. 150)

Thérèse gives this example: 'Once, I remember having left a cobweb in the cloister; [Mother Marie de Gonzague] said to me before the whole community: "We can easily see that our cloisters are swept by a child of fifteen! Go and take that cobweb away and be more careful in the future."' And continuing, Thérèse reports: 'During my postulancy, our Novice Mistress sent me each afternoon to weed the garden at 4:30. This cost me much since I was almost sure to meet Mother Marie de Gonzague. Once she said: "Really, this child does nothing at all! What sort of novice has to take a walk every day?"' Thérèse comments: 'She acted this way in everything concerning me' (SS, p. 150, n. 170).

Thérèse suffered greatly under the harsh discipline of Mother Marie de Gonzague. While not blind to her faults, though, Thérèse always showed a genuine affection and respect for her prioress. And she unfailingly accepted this often harsh treatment in a spirit of religious faith. Although frank and candid, she never spoke uncharitably about her prioress, nor did she ever imply that she was guilty of abuse or injustice.

If Marie de Gonzague was severe on Thérèse, it was also she who recognised the true spiritual mettle and potential greatness in her young charge. In her deposition to the tribunal for the beatification of Thérèse, Pauline testified:

Mother Marie de Gonzague, who was often very severe on [Thérèse], once told the novice-mistress, by way of explaining her attitude: 'Treating her like a child or being afraid to humiliate her at every turn is no way to handle a person of this calibre.' (Test, pp. 65-6)

And on the day after Thérèse's Profession, Marie de Gonzague wrote these words to the prioress of the Carmel of Tours:

> This angelic child is seventeen and a half, and she has the judgment of one of thirty, the religious perfection of an old perfected novice, and possession of herself; she is a perfect religious. Yesterday, not an eye remained dry at the sight of her great and entire immolation. (GC I, p. 678)

It was also Marie de Gonzague who recognised Thérèse's spiritual maturity and dared to appoint her, at the age of only 23, to assist her with forming the novices – a very bold and unconventional appointment for one so young. Thérèse confided to her: 'You didn't fear, dear Mother, that I would lead your little lambs astray. My lack of experience and my youthfulness did not frighten you in the least' (SS, p. 209). Thérèse was also the only one who dared to advise and console Mother Marie de Gonzague (cf. LT 190). The prioress, in turn, received and respected Thérèse's wisdom and affection.

4. Thérèse's Personality

Thérèse began life as a sickly child and was not expected to live. However, she survived and turned out to be bright, with a good memory. She writes, at the beginning of *Story of a Soul*: 'God granted me the favour of opening my intelligence at an early age and of imprinting childhood recollections so deeply on my memory that it seems the things I'm about to recount happened only yesterday' (SS, pp. 16-17). Considered 'a very intelligent student' by her teachers, the top of her class, she excelled especially at history, catechism and composition (cf. SS, pp. 81-2). At school, she acknowledges: 'I grasped easily the meaning of things I was learning, but I had trouble learning things word for word' (SS, p. 81). She also says that in her childhood she loved 'pictures and reading' (SS, p. 71), and that it was a cause of 'great sacrifices' (SS, p. 71) for her to stop reading at bedtime. It was through reading that she became inspired by the lives of French heroines, especially Joan of Arc, and desired to imitate them (cf. SS, p. 72).

Thérèse also had an affectionate heart, needing a lot of tenderness and love. She says: 'God was pleased all through my life to surround me with *love,* and the first memories I have are stamped with smiles and the most tender caresses. But although He placed so much *love* near me, He also sent much love into my little heart, making it warm and affectionate' (SS, p. 17). Looking back to her time at school, she acknowledges: 'My heart, sensitive and affectionate as it was, would have easily surrendered had it found a heart capable of understanding it… God gave me a heart which is so faithful that once it has loved purely, it loves always' (SS, pp. 82-3). Thérèse, then, had a great capacity for loving friendship. In her later years, it will become evident how she brought these qualities of her character to bear upon her vocation and her consecration to God, which characterises her loving fidelity.

In a letter, Zélie describes Thérèse as having 'a heart of gold', and the mother adds: 'she is very lovable and frank; it's curious to see her running after me making her confession: "Mama, I pushed Céline once, I hit her once, but I won't do it again."' (SS, p. 22). In another letter, Zélie again speaks of Thérèse's frankness, her transparency in conduct, and her need to be assured of forgiveness (cf. SS, pp. 18-19).

Thérèse also had a determined and stubborn personality. Her mother observes:

> Her intelligence is superior to Céline's, but she's less gentle and has a stubborn streak in her that is almost invincible; when she says '*no*' nothing can make her give in, and one could put her in the cellar a whole day and she'd sleep there rather than say 'yes'. (SS, p. 22)

And Thérèse recalls a childhood incident which she ascribes to her excessive self-love:

> One day, Mama said: 'Little Thérèse, if you kiss the ground I'll give you a sou.' A sou was a fortune at the time and to get it I didn't have to lower my dignity too much, my *little frame* didn't put much of a distance between my lips and the ground. And still my pride revolted at the thought of 'kissing the ground'; so standing up straight, I said to Mama: 'Oh! no, little Mother, I would prefer not to have the sou!' (SS, p. 24)

In *Story of a Soul*, Thérèse also testifies to her 'love of the good', and she gives credit to her parents and family for the way she was shaped and formed:

> With a nature such as my own, had I been reared by Parents without virtue or even if I had been spoiled by the maid, Louise, as Céline was, I would have become very bad and perhaps have even been lost.

But Jesus was watching over His little fiancée; He had willed that all turn out for her good, even her faults that, corrected very early, stood her in good stead to make her grow in perfection. As I had an excessive *self-love* and also a *love* of the *good*, as soon as I began to think seriously (which I did when still very little), it was enough for one to tell me a thing wasn't *good* and I had no desire to repeat it twice. (SS, pp. 24-5)

In the chapters that follow, the ways in which these personality traits played themselves out in her life will become apparent, as will other aspects of Thérèse's character.

II. Significant Events

Thérèse's life was not filled with extraordinary happenings. Indeed, she delighted in walking the ordinary ways of loving fidelity and generosity in her discipleship of Jesus. Three important events do stand out, however. They will be referred to again later, but for now are introduced here: her First Communion, her Christmas Grace, and her Act of Oblation to Merciful Love.

1. First Communion

Thérèse's First Communion on May 8, 1884, at the age of 11, was a profoundly significant event in her life. She speaks of it in terms of the consummation of a long-desired relationship of intimacy with Jesus. She expresses it in terms of marital love, as a transition from a 'look' to a 'fusion'. This language connotes the deepening and maturing of the relationship, from that of an engagement to one of marriage. This is how she describes the event:

> Ah! how sweet was that first kiss of Jesus! It was a kiss of *love*; I *felt* that *I was loved*, and I said: 'I love You, and I give myself to You forever!' There were no demands made, no struggles, no sacrifices; for a long time now Jesus and poor little Thérèse *looked at* and understood each other. That day, it was no longer simply a *look*, it was a fusion; they were no longer two, Thérèse had vanished as a drop of water is lost in the immensity of the ocean. Jesus alone remained; He was the Master, the King. (SS, p. 77)

2. The Christmas Grace

This event, which occurred on December 25, 1886 when Thérèse was 13, was a powerful turning point in her life. She refers to this occurrence as 'the grace of my complete conversion' (SS, p. 98). It liberated her from the hypersensitivity which had been afflicting her for ten years and which, all this time, she had been struggling to overcome. It was such a momentous happening for Thérèse that she could remember the exact date, time and place, and all the other details about it. This is how she describes it:

> It was December 25, 1886...We [Louis, Céline and Thérèse] had come back from Midnight Mass where I had the happiness of receiving the *strong* and *powerful* God. Upon arriving at Les Buissonnets, I used to love to take my shoes from the chimney corner and examine the presents in them; this old custom had given us so much joy in our youth that Céline wanted to continue treating me as a baby since I was

the youngest in the family. Papa had always loved to see my happiness and listen to my cries of delight as I drew each surprise from the *magic shoes*, and my dear King's gaiety increased my own happiness very much. However, Jesus desired to show me that I was to give up the defects of my childhood and so He withdrew its innocent pleasures. He permitted Papa, tired out after the Midnight Mass, to experience annoyance when seeing my shoes at the fireplace, and that he speak those words which pierced my heart: 'Well, fortunately, this will be the last year!' I was going upstairs, at the time, to remove my hat, and Céline, knowing how sensitive I was and seeing the tears already glistening in my eyes, wanted to cry too, for she loved me very much and understood my grief. She said, 'Oh, Thérèse, don't go downstairs; it would cause you too much grief to look at your slippers right now!' But Thérèse was no longer the same; Jesus had changed her heart! Forcing back my tears, I descended the stairs rapidly; controlling the poundings of my heart, I took my slippers and placed them in front of Papa, and withdrew all the objects joyfully. I had the happy appearance of a Queen. Having regained his own cheerfulness, Papa was laughing; Céline believed it was all a *dream*! Fortunately, it was a sweet reality; Thérèse had discovered once again the strength of soul which she had lost at the age of four and a half, and she was to preserve it forever! (SS, p. 98)

3. Act of Oblation to Merciful Love

In keeping with the religious ethos of the time, the convent of Lisieux was also infected with Jansenism.

This heresy so emphasised the justice and holiness of God that it neglected God's mercy and love. Many of the nuns in the convent were offering themselves as victims to God's justice 'in order to turn away the punishments reserved to sinners, drawing them upon themselves' (SS, p. 180). Acknowledging their great generosity of soul, Thérèse, nevertheless, confesses that she felt no attraction to emulate the sisters in their self-offering to God's justice.

Then, on June 9, 1895, the Feast of the Holy Trinity, Thérèse received a special grace to understand how much Jesus desired to be loved. And so, in order to satisfy Jesus' 'Merciful Love', she sought and received a special permission from her prioress (who at that time was her sister Pauline) to offer herself as a victim to God's Merciful Love. Speaking to God about her self-offering, Thérèse cries out:

O my God! Will Your Justice alone find souls willing to immolate themselves as victims? Does not Your *Merciful Love* need them too?... It seems to me that if You were to find souls offering themselves as victims of holocaust to Your Love, You would consume them rapidly; it seems to me, too, that You would be happy not to hold back the waves of infinite tenderness within You. If Your Justice loves to release itself, this Justice *which extends only over the earth*, how much more does Your Merciful Love desire to *set souls on fire* since Your Mercy *reaches to the heavens*. O my Jesus, let me be this happy victim; consume Your holocaust with the fire of Your Divine Love!' (SS, pp. 180-1)

This is the very heart of Thérèse's whole spirituality.

Chapter Two

THE WRITINGS

For someone who died at only 24, and who spent just nine years in the Carmel of Lisieux, Thérèse has left us a considerable body of works. We can look now at her major writings[1] so as to explore their *nature* and *content*, their *origin*, and how they came to the *attention of the public*. As we will focus mainly on *Story of a Soul*, we will first examine her letters and the *Last Conversations*.

I. Letters

There are 266 letters of Thérèse which have been preserved. They date from the age of four, in 1877, right up to her death 20 years later. It is evident from her letters that Thérèse was a good correspondent – she seems to have enjoyed communicating. Her letters are never hastily written, but carefully planned and well thought out. They are addressed to a wide range of people, the majority being to the members of her immediate family, relatives and friends, and to her two missionary brothers, Père Roulland and Abbé Bellière,[2] who were committed to Thérèse's spiritual care.

The letters are interesting from many points of view. Not only do they contain Thérèse's doctrine and spirituality, but they also reveal her personality, her interests and concerns, and her ability to advise and console. And given the nature of these documents –

written to individuals and reflecting the particular relationship and the person's concerns – there is an appealing spontaneity, intimacy and immediacy. Furthermore, if we read through them in chronological order, the letters enable us to trace Thérèse's psychological and spiritual development. They also show us recurrent ideas and themes, and how they developed in the course of her life.

II. Last Conversations

The *Last Conversations* are not the writings of Thérèse herself. However, they can be considered a sequel to *Story of a Soul.* They consist of personal recollections of conversations with Thérèse during the last few months of her life, while she was confined to the infirmary. These jottings, which date from April to September 1897, were recorded by Thérèse's sisters Pauline, Marie and Céline, as well as some of the nuns who were close to the saint. Here, we see Thérèse's ability to counsel and encourage those who were troubled or struggling, and we also gain an insight into her personal reflections in the face of terrible physical and spiritual sufferings, leading up to her death.

'When we are reading her words,' writes the editor of the *Last Conversations*, 'we can almost sense her presence at our side, speaking directly to us, sharing with us her human experience, her joys, her sufferings, her views on a variety of topics, her love for God, and especially her trust in Him in spite of her terrible ordeal' (LC, p. 7). Here are two sample extracts that give a flavour of this work – one from the beginning, on silence in the face of judgment, and one from the end, on her approaching death.

April 6, 1897: The possible context of this extract is Pauline confiding to Thérèse her hurt feelings at being unjustly judged in community by one of the nuns. Thérèse advises:

> When we're misunderstood and judged unfavourably, what good does it do to defend or explain ourselves? Let the matter drop and say nothing. It's so much better to say nothing and allow others to judge us as they please! We don't see in the Gospel where Mary explained herself when her sister accused her of remaining at Jesus' feet, doing nothing! She didn't say: 'Oh, Martha, if you only knew the joy I am experiencing, if you only heard the words I hear! And besides, it's Jesus who told me to remain here.' No, she preferred to remain silent. O blessed silence that gives so much peace to souls! (LC, p. 36)

September 11, 1897: Here, the context may be Pauline asking Thérèse about her feelings towards her imminent death. Thérèse replies:

> I'm afraid I've feared death, but I won't fear it after it takes place; I'm sure of this! And I'm not sorry for having lived; oh! no. It's only when I ask myself: What is this mysterious separation of the soul from the body? It's my first experience of this, but I abandon myself to God. (LC, p. 188)

III. Story of a Soul

This work is undoubtedly the best-known of Thérèse's writings. It is an account of her life, into which are woven her doctrine and spirituality. *Story of a Soul* is often referred to as an autobiography; but while this is partly true, we need to explain this further.

Story of a Soul is not a single manuscript in which Thérèse provides a sustained account of her life. Although she speaks of her childhood, her family and her experiences in the convent, *Story of a Soul* can more accurately be described as a *spiritual* autobiography. Indeed, every account of a life is written from a particular viewpoint and emerges from a specific context.

In *Story of a Soul* Thérèse recounts and interprets the facts and experiences of her life from a predominantly (though not exclusively) religious or spiritual point of view. Her life is told from the perspective of her Christian faith, her life understood primarily in the context of her relationship with God. For Thérèse, this relationship is characterised by his merciful love towards her. Hence, she acknowledges at the beginning: 'I'm going to be doing only one thing: I shall begin to sing what I must sing eternally: *"The Mercies of the Lord"*' (SS, p. 13; cf. p. 205).

Story of a Soul is not a single piece of work that Thérèse composed from beginning to end. Written over a period of about three years, it consists of three separate manuscripts, each of them addressed to a different person, in response to a different request, and at a different time. These writings are known, respectively, as Manuscripts A, B and C.

1. Manuscript A

The first manuscript is dated 'January 1895' and is entitled by Thérèse, 'Springtime story of a little white flower written by herself and dedicated to the Reverend

Mother Agnes of Jesus' (SS, p. 13). Mother Agnes who, as we have seen, was Thérèse's sister Pauline, was prioress at the Lisieux convent from 1893 to 1896 – and again after Thérèse's death. It begins with the following statement:

> It is to you, dear Mother, to you who are doubly my Mother, that I come to confide the story of my soul. The day you asked me to do this, it seemed to me it would distract my heart by too much concentration on myself, but since then Jesus has made me feel that in obeying simply, I would be pleasing Him... (SS, p. 13)

So it is clear that, in spite of an initial reluctance, Thérèse is writing in response to a request and out of obedience.

How did this manuscript come to be composed? What prompted Mother Agnes to order Thérèse to write? The background is clearly documented in Pauline's testimony:

> As for how [Thérèse] came to write her life-story, it was like this: one winter's evening early in 1895 (two and a half years before Sister Thérèse's death), I was chatting with my two sisters, Marie and Thérèse, and the latter was telling us a lot of stories about her childhood. 'Mother,' said Sister Marie of the Sacred Heart, 'what a pity we haven't got all that in writing! If you asked Sister Thérèse of the Child Jesus to write down her childhood memories for us, I am sure we'd find them very entertaining.' 'I couldn't ask for anything better,' I replied. Then I turned to Sister Thérèse, who was laughing at what she took to be a bit of leg-pulling, and said, 'I order

you to write down all your childhood memories.'
(Test, p. 33)

Manuscript A, then, resulted from an informal family conversation among the three Martin sisters during which Thérèse was reminiscing about her childhood past.

Who were the intended readers? Céline testifies that Manuscript A was 'really a family souvenir, and meant only for her sisters' (Test, p. 121). She goes on to say: 'That explains its easy familiarity and the inclusion of certain details of her childhood that she might have baulked at, if she had foreseen that the manuscript would leave the family circle' (Test, p. 121).

So, Manuscript A was not written for the eyes of the general public, but solely for the intimate circle of the Martin family. In other words, Thérèse had no idea that her manuscript would reach a worldwide audience. If she had known, maybe she would have revealed less of herself. Instead, we have a simple, uncontrived, candid outpouring of Thérèse's thoughts and reflections on her life.

Céline also testifies: '[Thérèse] only wrote off and on, in the rare moments of leisure allowed her by the rule and her work with the novices. She wrote as it came to her, without any rough draft, and yet her manuscript contains no erasures' (Test, p. 121). Therefore, although Thérèse was under obedience to write an account of her childhood memories, additional time was not granted to accomplish this task. She had to find time for it.

Pauline reports that Thérèse completed this manuscript on January 20, 1896 – about a year after she had begun writing it:

She wrote only during her free time, and gave me her copy-book on my feastday – 20 January, 1896. I was at evening prayer, and she gave it to me as she passed my stall on the way to her own. I acknowledged it with a nod, and put it down beside me without opening it. In fact, I did not get round to reading it until after the elections in the Spring. I noticed the Servant of God's virtue with regard to this: once she had done what obedience had required, she thought no more of it, and never even asked me if I had read it or what I thought of it. One day I told her that I had not had time to read it; she did not seem the slightest bit offended. (Test, p. 33)

Manuscript A contains Thérèse's life from the time of her childhood right up to her entry into the Lisieux convent. She does not recount much here about her life in Carmel – she followed her brief, which was to write down her 'childhood memories'. In this account, we see Thérèse distinguishing 'three separate periods' (SS, p. 16) in her life.

*

The **first period**, she says, 'is not the least fruitful in memories in spite of its short duration. It extends from the dawn of my reason till our dear Mother's departure for Heaven' (SS, p. 16). This period of Thérèse's life, up to the age of four, was a very happy one. She acknowledges: 'Oh! everything truly smiled upon me on this earth: I found flowers under each of my steps and my happy disposition contributed much to making life pleasant' (SS, p. 30). However, already a portentous event was in the making. She continues: 'but a new period was about to commence for my soul.

41

I had to pass through the crucible of trial and to suffer from my childhood in order to be offered earlier to Jesus' (SS, p. 30).

*

The **second period**, she tells us, 'extends from the age of four and a half [that is, the death of her mother] to that of fourteen, the time when I found once again my *childhood* character, and entered more and more into the serious side of life' (SS, p. 34). Zélie's death was a major traumatic blow to Thérèse, occasioning a profound change in her character and temperament. She writes:

> my happy disposition completely changed after Mama's death. I, once so full of life, became timid and retiring, sensitive to an excessive degree. One look was enough to reduce me to tears, and the only way I was content was to be left alone completely. I could not bear the company of strangers and found my joy only within the intimacy of the family. (SS, pp. 34-5)

This second period was 'the most painful of the three' (SS, p. 34). It included the departures of both Pauline (1882) and Marie (1886) for the convent, which left Thérèse feeling abandoned and emotionally bereft. These distressing events contributed to her mysterious illness, which was cured by the Virgin Mary who looked on her with a *'ravishing smile'* (SS, p. 66). This was also the period when she suffered from scruples (cf. SS, p. 88) and was unhappy at school – the time which she refers to as 'the saddest in my life' (SS, p. 53).

*

The **third period** began on December 25, 1886, when 'I received the grace of leaving my childhood, in a word, the grace of my complete conversion' (SS, p. 98). As we have seen, this 'Christmas grace' was so powerful that Thérèse remembers the precise date, time and place (her return from Midnight Mass). She was now almost 14, and she calls this next period 'the most beautiful and the most filled with graces from heaven'. She continues: 'The work I had been unable to do in ten years was done by Jesus in one instant, contenting himself with my *good will* which was never lacking' (SS, p. 98). This grace liberated Thérèse from her struggles to overcome her excessive sensitivity and immaturity, which, she confesses, had been making her 'really unbearable' (SS, p. 97).

It is important to recognise that Thérèse did not sit back complacently during the ten years when she was afflicted with hypersensitivity, and wait for God's grace to transform and heal her. On the contrary, she kept on trying, doing her best, to overcome her defects. And her efforts were rewarded in due time. Hence, while an important principle of Thérèse's spirituality is 'ALL is grace!' (cf. LC, p. 57), this must be understood properly. What it means, at least for Thérèse, is not that we should do nothing and God everything, but that there is no proportion between our genuine, little, stumbling efforts at conversion – our cooperation with God – and the transformation that God finally brings about.

2. Manuscript B

The second manuscript is dated 'September 8, 1896' – about a year and three weeks before Thérèse's death. It is addressed: 'To my dear Sister Marie of the Sacred Heart' (SS, p. 190). Manuscript B consists of an accompanying letter addressed to her sister Marie, and the main text which is written in the form of a letter to Jesus.

In the letter to Marie, Thérèse says: 'When writing these words, I shall address them to Jesus since this makes it easier for me to express my thoughts' (SS, p. 189). This reveals much about Thérèse's relationship with Jesus. We express our thoughts and feelings most readily and easily to a person with whom we feel comfortable, able to be intimate. With strangers, we tend to be more hesitant and guarded in our communication and behaviour. So we see that Thérèse is most at home with Jesus, whom she calls '*my first and only Friend*, You whom *I love* UNIQUELY' (SS, p. 197).

Manuscript B is by far the shortest of the three manuscripts, and considered 'the jewel of all Thérèse's writings' (SS, p. xvii). She tells Marie how this manuscript came to be composed: 'O my dear Sister! you ask me to give you a souvenir of my retreat, one which will probably be my last... O my dear Sister, you wish to hear about the secrets Jesus confides to your little sister' (SS, p. 187). This manuscript, then, was written solely for Marie, at her request. And what does it contain? Again, Thérèse tells us: 'You asked me, dear Sister, to write to you *my dream* and "*my little doctrine*" as you call it. I did this in these following pages' (SS, p. 189). These pages are an expression of her spiritual doctrine – the burning heart of Thérèse's Little Way.

There are many beautiful thoughts and insights into Thérèse's spiritual doctrine in this manuscript. Above all, Thérèse reveals here how she came to discover the essence of her vocation and mission: to be '*Love* in the heart of the Church' (cf. SS, p. 194).

3. Manuscript C

The third manuscript is dated 'June 1897' (SS, p. 205) – less than four months before Thérèse's death. It is addressed to Mother Marie de Gonzague, who had succeeded Pauline as prioress on March 21, 1896. Again, Thérèse discloses why she wrote this manuscript: 'You have told me, my dear Mother, of your desire that I finish *singing* with you the *Mercies of the Lord*. I began this sweet song with your dear daughter, Agnes of Jesus, who was the mother entrusted by God with guiding me in the days of my childhood' (SS, p. 205). Pauline also testifies to how this manuscript came into being. She says that, after reading Manuscript A:

> I found her account incomplete. She had dwelt on her childhood and early youth, as I had asked, but had dealt with her religious life only in barest outline. I thought it a pity that she had not treated her religious life in the same detail, but I was then no longer prioress – Mother Gonzague had returned to that office. I was afraid the latter would not be so interested in this manuscript as I was, and I dared not mention it to her. Then Sister Thérèse became seriously ill, and I decided to try the impossible. Towards midnight on 2 June, 1897, four months before Sister Thérèse's death, I went to Mother Prioress's room and said: 'Mother, I cannot sleep until I tell you a certain secret. While I was prioress, Sister Thérèse wrote some memoirs of her childhood. She did so out of obedience and to please me. The

45

other day I read them through again, and they are very charming, but they will not be of much use to you when it comes to writing her obituary letter because she says hardly anything about her life as a nun. Now, if you were to order her to do so, she could write something a little more serious, and I am sure it would be much better than the manuscript I have.' (Test, pp. 33-4)

Pauline goes on to affirm: 'God blessed my endeavour: the following morning Mother Gonzague ordered Sister Thérèse to continue her account' (Test, p. 34).

From this testimony it is evident that one of the purposes of this manuscript was to supply information for Thérèse's 'circular', the obituary letter sent to other Carmels after a nun's death. Unlike Manuscripts A and B, Manuscript C was never completed. The last sentence reads: 'It is not because God, in His anticipating Mercy, has preserved my soul from mortal sin that I go to Him with confidence and love...' (SS, p. 259). Even this sentence is incomplete. It is reported that at this point Thérèse was too weak to continue. She could no longer manage to hold a pencil in her hand.

Manuscript C covers mainly Thérèse's life in Carmel, as the prioress had requested. It contains some of her richest insights into the Scriptures, especially with regard to the nature of Christian charity. In this manuscript Thérèse also speaks of her 'night of faith', of her struggles to live authentically her religious vows, of challenges faced in community living, of her search for the 'divine elevator', of prayer, and of her work with the novices; here, too, she introduces her two spiritual brothers, Roulland and Bellière.

IV. A Grace of God's Providence

It is clear that Thérèse did not write these three manuscripts in order to communicate her special doctrine to the world. As has been seen, they were written in response to a request, or in obedience to the then prioress. Thérèse was very particular about this manner of proceeding, not only with regard to her autobiography but also with regard to letters. She writes: 'I feel that if my letters are to do any good they must be written under obedience, and that I should feel repugnance rather than pleasure in writing them' (SS, p. 252; cf. LC, p. 82).

This attitude is confirmed by Thérèse's reaction to Sr Marie of the Trinity, one of her novices, who expressed a wish to write a memoir of her own vocation. Thérèse replied:

> Beware of doing anything of the kind!... Anyway, you cannot do it without permission, and I advise you not to ask for it. I certainly would not like to write anything about my life without a special order to do so, and an unasked-for order at that. It is more in keeping with humility to write nothing about yourself. The great graces of life, such as a vocation, cannot be forgotten, and they will do more good when recalled to mind than when read about on paper. (Test, p. 250)

The initiative in writing *Story of a Soul*, then, did not come from Thérèse, and her motive was not publication. As we have seen, Manuscript A was written for the Martin family, B for her sister Marie, and C for her obituary 'circular'.

However, there now comes a surprising turn of

events! Towards the end of her life, Thérèse had a strange presentiment about her writings. She came to believe that she had a 'mission' to teach people her spirituality, her way to God. On July 17, 1897 – just 12 weeks before her death – Thérèse said to Pauline: 'I feel that I'm about to enter into my rest. But I feel especially that my mission is about to begin, my mission of making God loved as I love Him, of giving my little way to souls' (LC, p. 102). And in her testimony during the enquiry process for Thérèse's beatification, Pauline recounts the following conversation, in which Thérèse has begun to see the importance of her writings:

> *Thérèse:* The manuscript [her autobiography] must be published without delay after my death. If you delay, the devil will set all sorts of traps to stop its publication, important though it is.
> *Pauline:* So you think it is by means of the manuscript that you are going to benefit people?
> *Thérèse:* Yes, it is one of the means which God will use to make me heard. It will benefit all kinds of people, except those who travel by extraordinary ways.
> *Pauline:* But what if Mother Prioress throws it in the fire?
> *Thérèse:* That's all right. It won't hurt me in the least, or make me doubt my mission in the slightest. I would merely think that God was going to satisfy my desires in some other way. (Test, p. 64; cf. LC, pp. 126 & 143)

Today, *Story of a Soul* belongs to the whole Church. And the fact that it was written not on her own initiative or with the intention of publication, but under obedience, is a grace of God's providence. In the three manuscripts, Thérèse has unwittingly left to the world her spiritual doctrine of the Little Way – the way of absolute trust, confidence, and surrender to God, as she came to develop it and live it out in the concrete situation of her community life.

What is striking, as we read through *Story of a Soul*, is the spiritual genius of this 24-year-old. This is evident in the boldness, courage and conviction with which she speaks. It is especially, perhaps, her 'sureness of touch' that manifests her genius. Thérèse is like a violin prodigy who plays with confidence, not having to 'feel' for the notes. Her message has an undeniable ring of truth.

We might end by asking: What did Thérèse think of *Story of a Soul*? These are the words of Pauline, two months before Thérèse's death:

A few days later, having asked her to read again a passage of her manuscript which seemed incomplete to me, I found her crying. When I asked her why, she answered with angelic simplicity:

'What I am reading in this copybook reflects my soul so well! Mother, these pages will do much good to souls. They will understand God's gentleness much better.' (LC, p. 126)

Chapter Three

THE SCRIPTURES

The Bible is the Christian's most sacred and privileged document. It is the book of the Church, the book of the people of God, and the source of Christian revelation. We turn to the Scriptures to discover who God is, what he is like, and how he wishes us to live in relationship with him and with others. Vatican II emphasised the special nature of the Scriptures in *Dei Verbum*, the *Dogmatic Constitution on Divine Revelation*: 'Sacred Scripture is the speech of God as it is put down in writing under the breath of the Holy Spirit' (DV 9).

One of the many blessings that has flowed from the Second Vatican Council has been a renewed emphasis on the Scriptures and a deeper appreciation of their importance for a life of prayer and discipleship. In *Dei Verbum*, for example, we read:

> 'Ignorance of the Scriptures is ignorance of Christ.' [St Jerome] Therefore, let [the Christian faithful] go gladly to the sacred text itself, whether in the sacred liturgy, which is full of the divine words, or in devout reading... Let them remember, however, that prayer should accompany the reading of sacred Scripture, so that a dialogue takes place between God and man. For, 'we speak to him when we pray; we listen to him when we read the divine oracles.' [St Ambrose] (DV 25)

Hence, Vatican II affirms these two points: firstly, that Scripture is a necessary and privileged source of knowledge about Jesus – and therefore about God as revealed in and through Jesus; and secondly, that God speaks to us through his word. In short, knowledge of the Scriptures is crucial for authentic Christian discipleship.

Thérèse was, in a way, unusual for her times: she did not have easy access to the Bible as we do today, yet she lived out the invitation of the Council to read, ponder and pray the Scriptures. They were, as we shall see, central to her life, and of paramount importance in her spiritual growth and development.

I. The Scriptures in the Life of Thérèse

1. A Great Love of Scripture

From her own account it is clear that Thérèse had a great love for the Scriptures. She was not content with a superficial knowledge of them. On the contrary, she had a profound desire to penetrate into the very truth of the word of God. This is evident from a conversation with Pauline, just six weeks before Thérèse's death:

> It's only in heaven that we'll see the whole truth about everything. This is impossible on earth. Thus, even regarding Holy Scripture, isn't it sad to see so many different translations! Had I been a priest, I would have learned Hebrew and Greek, and wouldn't have been satisfied with Latin. In this way, I would have known the real text dictated by the Holy Spirit. (LC, p. 132)

And Céline recalls that Thérèse wished she could have studied Hebrew and Greek 'in order to know the divine thinking exactly as God deigned to express it in human language' (Test, p. 123).

We can see how well Thérèse knew the Scriptures from the number of times she refers to and quotes from them, and also from the diversity of the biblical books she uses. It was pointed out by John Paul II that her writings contain more than 400 quotations from the Old Testament and over 600 from the New.[1] *Story of a Soul* itself has more than 130 biblical quotations, in addition to a large number of allusions to the Scriptures. As we can see, Thérèse drew copiously on both the Old and the New Testaments. In *Story of a Soul*, for instance, she quotes or alludes to no fewer than 14 books of the Old Testament.[2] As for the New Testament, while she draws chiefly on the Gospels, there are also passages from seven other books.[3] It seems that the Psalms, the Song of Songs, and the Gospels of Luke and John were among her favourites.

Given that Thérèse had no formal study of the Scriptures, that her time for private reading in the convent was limited due to work and sickness, that her access to the Bible, especially the Old Testament, was restricted, and that she died at only 24, her great familiarity with Scripture is actually quite astonishing.

2. A Book that Paved the Way

Thérèse also reveals that up to the time of her entry into Carmel, she was not familiar with the Scriptures. Speaking of herself at the age of 14, she says: 'I was nourished for a long time on the "pure flour" contained in the Imitation of Christ, this being the only book which did me any good, for as yet I had not discovered the treasures hidden in the Gospels' (SS, p. 102). At this stage in her life, she was inseparable from *The Imitation of Christ*: 'This little book never parted company with me, for in summer I carried it in my pocket, in winter, in my muff' (SS, p. 102). She knew this work of Thomas à Kempis so well that, no matter where she opened the book, she could recite by heart to the end of the chapter.

The Imitation of Christ is steeped in references to the Scriptures, and Thérèse would undoubtedly have absorbed many biblical texts from it. In her spiritual development, then, the *Imitation* acted as a preparation for introducing her to the word of God. So we can ask: What does this book teach about the Bible? We have, for example, this passage in the chapter, 'About Reading the Holy Scripture' (bk. I, ch. 5):

> It is for truth, not for literary excellence, that we go to Holy Scripture; every passage of it ought to be read in the light of that inspiration which produced it, with an eye to our soul's profit, not to cleverness of argument... Mankind is always changing; God's truth stands for ever. And he has many ways of speaking to us, regardless of the human instruments he uses. Often enough, our reading of Holy Scripture is distracted by mere curiosity; we want to seize upon a point and argue about it, when we ought to be quietly passing on. You will get most out of it if you read it with humility, and simplicity, and faith, not concerned to make a name for yourself as a scholar. By all means ask questions, but listen to what holy writers have to tell you; do not find fault with the hard sayings of antiquity – their authors had good reason for writing as they did.[4]

It is not surprising, then, given her familiarity with the *Imitation,* that Thérèse's manner of reading the Scriptures follows the attitudes and dispositions recommended by this work. It will become evident that she reads the divine text with humility, simplicity and faith, and reads not so as to argue about it but to discover the truth for her soul's profit.

The other spiritual writings that Thérèse found especially helpful in her spiritual growth were those of John of the Cross. She writes:

> Ah! how many lights have I not drawn from the works of our holy Father, St. John of the Cross! At the ages of seventeen and eighteen I had no other spiritual nourishment; later on, however, all books left me in aridity and I'm still in that state. If I open a book composed by a spiritual author (even the most beautiful, the most touching book), I feel my heart contract immediately and I read without understanding, so to speak. Or if I do understand, my mind comes to a standstill without the capacity of meditating. (SS, p. 179)

Thérèse goes on to recount what she did in this period of aridity, when she could not find any nourishment in spiritual books – and she is now at her most mature stage of development:

> In this helplessness, Holy Scripture and the Imitation come to my aid; in them I discover a solid and very *pure* nourishment. But it is especially the *Gospels* that sustain me during my hours of prayer, for in them I find what is necessary for my poor little soul. I am constantly discovering in them new lights, hidden and mysterious meanings. (SS, p. 179)[5]

So, when all other books failed to provide spiritual sustenance, it was the Scriptures, and especially the Gospels, that sustained Thérèse. With regard to the 'new lights, hidden and mysterious meanings', Sr Marie of the Trinity testified at the diocesan process: 'I am very sorry that I did not note down systematically all the lights which she received in prayer and passed on to me for the good of my soul. She had an extraordinary ability for interpreting the Scriptures. She was so good at discovering all the beauty of these holy books that it was as if they no longer held any secrets for her' (Test, p. 236).

3. Steeped in the Gospels

Thérèse was inseparable from the Gospels, and Céline has this to say:

> She even carried this sacred book [the Gospels] around next to her heart, and used to go to considerable trouble to find editions of the individual gospels, which she then bound together so that others could do as she did. She studied the Bible 'in order to find out what God was like'. (Test, p. 122)

In this last phrase Céline is quoting Thérèse's own words.

Thérèse once wrote: 'the book of the Gospels…never leaves me' (LT 193; cf. MSST, p. 108). Her familiarity with them can be seen in an episode recalled by Pauline, only about a fortnight before Thérèse's death. Pauline writes: 'It was the feast of the Holy Name of Mary. She asked me to read her the Sunday Gospel. I didn't have the missal and told her simply: "It's the Gospel where Our Lord warns us against serving two

55

masters." [Mt 6:24-33] Then, imitating the voice of a little child reciting her lesson, she said it from memory from beginning to end' (LC, pp. 188-9). And Céline recalls:

At Carmel the Bible was her greatest treasure, and it was with amazing ease and keen perception that she was able to assimilate various passages of [Holy Scripture]; she found no difficulty in discovering their hidden meaning and then in applying the lesson in a very unusual way. (MSST, p. 107)

Sr Marie of the Trinity gives this testimony: 'She also had a filial love of St Teresa and St John of the Cross. The latter's writing especially filled her with love. But it was the Scriptures, and the Gospel above all, that she constantly cited, and to such good effect that you might say her conversations were a commentary on the Bible' (Test, p. 242). Thérèse, then, had imbibed the Scriptures so well, and the word of God had become so much part of her being, that she spoke out of it without even having consciously to think about it.

For Thérèse, the Scriptures, and especially the Gospels, were her privileged and immediate contact with God, and with God's Word, Jesus. In and through the divine words she discovered the God she so much desired and loved. Commenting on a favourite line of hers from the Song of Songs (Sg 1:3-4), 'Draw me; we shall run after you in the odour of your ointments', Thérèse reflects: 'Since Jesus has reascended into heaven, I can follow Him only in the traces He has left; but how luminous these traces are! how perfumed! I have only to cast a glance in the Gospels and immediately I breathe in the perfumes of Jesus' life, and I know on which side to run' (SS, p. 258).

The Scriptures became Thérèse's ultimate teacher and guide in her spiritual journey. In them, and particularly in the Gospels, she discovered the will of Jesus, which enabled her to learn how to live out her relationship with him. In *Story of a Soul*, commenting on the verse from Matthew, 'It is not those who say: "Lord, Lord!" who will enter the kingdom of heaven, but those who do the will of my Father in heaven' (Mt 7:21), she comments: 'Jesus has revealed this will several times or I should say on almost every page of His Gospel' (SS, p. 219).

As the Scriptures were her privileged means of access to Jesus, it is not surprising that Thérèse came to abandon all other books so as to devote herself entirely to the study of the word of God. This comes across clearly in the following incident. On May 15, 1897, Pauline says: 'I was speaking to her about certain practices of devotion and perfection counselled by the saints, which were a source of discouragement to me' (LC, p. 43). Thérèse replied: 'As for me, with the exception of the Gospels, I no longer find anything in books. The Gospels are enough. I listen with delight to these words of Jesus which tell me all I must do: "Learn of me for I am meek and humble of heart"; then I'm at peace, according to His sweet promise: "and you will find rest for your souls"' (LC, p. 44). Thérèse had a similar remedy for Fr Roulland, who was afraid of God's justice. She wrote to him:

I do not understand souls who fear a Friend so tender. At times, when I am reading certain spiritual treatises in which perfection is shown through a thousand obstacles, surrounded by a crowd of illusions, my poor little mind quickly tires; I close the learned book that is breaking my head and drying up my heart, and I take up Holy Scripture. Then all seems luminous to me; a single word uncovers for my soul infinite horizons, perfection seems simple to me, I see it is sufficient to recognise one's nothingness and to abandon oneself as a child into God's arms. (LT 226)

As Thérèse says so well, the Gospels provide all that is necessary for discipleship and salvation. Unlike some spiritual books that make the journey to God appear arduous and difficult, leaving us feeling discouraged or even excluded, Jesus does not make it difficult for those who desire to come to him.

Ultimately, the Scriptures defined and gave form to Thérèse's life. The Gospels especially became her rule of life. All other spiritual books and writings took her only so far, but left her unsatisfied. In reading the Gospels, however, she encountered Jesus himself – he who is the Word of God – and she heard the words of him who is the Way, the Truth and the Life.

II. Thérèse's Use of Scripture

So far, we have seen how important the Scriptures are in Thérèse's life. But how does she *use* them? How does Thérèse interpret the word of God in, and for, her life?

The first thing to note is that Thérèse knew nothing of scriptural exegesis and did not read the Bible as a scholar, looking objectively for the literal meaning. On the contrary, she read the Scriptures subjectively, in a way that was primarily *prayerful* (with the spirit of faith), *personal* (as a word addressed to her), and *existential* (addressing her present circumstances). And she brought with her the dispositions advocated in *The Imitation of Christ*: humility, simplicity and faith, so as to discover the truth for the benefit of her soul. In the examples which follow, we can see the ways in which Thérèse read the sacred text.

1. Life Illumined by Scripture

The first example marks the beginning of *Story of a Soul*. When Pauline told her to record her early memories, this is how Thérèse proceeded:

> Before taking up my pen, I knelt before the statue of Mary...and I begged her to guide my hand that it trace no line displeasing to her. Then opening the Holy Gospels my eyes fell on these words: 'And going up a mountain, he called to him men of his *own choosing*, and they came to him' (St. Mark, chap. III, v.13). (SS, p. 13)

So, after an initial prayer for Mary's assistance, Thérèse immediately goes to the Scriptures for guidance and inspiration. In coming upon the text from Mark, she interprets it personally, applying it to her own life and vocation. Thérèse is not, of course, a 'man' but can identify herself as one of those 'men', the disciples, called by Jesus. She exclaims – and note her 'my', used here three times: 'This is the mystery of my vocation, my whole life, and especially the mystery of the privileges Jesus showered on my soul' (SS, p. 13). As far as Thérèse is concerned, this passage from Mark illumines her own call, her experience of being chosen by Jesus.

Another example occurs when Thérèse replies to a letter from Céline, in distress because of the intensity of her spiritual aridity. Thérèse writes:

> After having read your letter, I went to prayer, and taking the gospel, I asked Jesus to find a passage for you, and this is what I found: 'Behold the fig tree and the other trees, when they begin to bear tender leaves, you judge that summer is near. In the same way, when you will see these things taking place, know that the kingdom of God is near.' [Lk 21:29-31] I closed the book, I had read enough; in fact, *these things* taking place in my Céline's soul prove the kingdom of Jesus is set up in her soul... (LT 143)

Here again, Thérèse prays, and then immediately turns to the word of God, in a spirit of faith, to obtain an answer. She is also confident that the passage she alights on is appropriate for Céline's situation. And so she interprets her sister's struggles in the light of the gospel text, concluding that the experiences of spiritual aridity ('these things') are proof that the kingdom of God is coming to birth in Céline's soul.

On another occasion, Thérèse was in deep gloom about her life and vocation and 'wondering whether God was really pleased with me' (LC, p. 49). While in this mood, she received a chance note from Pauline in which, as Thérèse says:

> You were telling me that everything in me pleased you, that I was especially loved by God, that He had not made me, as He did others, climb the rough ladder of perfection, but that he had placed me in an elevator so that I might be brought to Him more speedily. (LC, p. 49)

This is how Thérèse describes her reaction: 'Already, I was much touched, but always the thought that your love made you see what wasn't there hindered me from rejoicing fully' (LC, p. 49). Although she appreciated Pauline's affirmation, nevertheless Thérèse was concerned that Pauline's love for her may have blinded her to the truth of her younger sister's real spiritual condition.

Thérèse recounts how she resolved the issue: 'Then I took my little Gospels, asking God to console me, to answer me Himself, and my glance fell upon this passage which I'd never noticed before: "For he whom God sent speaks the words of God, for not by measure does God give the Spirit" [Jn 3:34]' (LC, p. 49). She recognised Pauline's note in the light of this passage, and confidently concluded: 'It is you, little Mother, whom God has sent for me... You speak the same words as God, and now I believe that God is very much content with me since you have said so' (LC, p. 49). So, Thérèse's consolation came not primarily from Pauline's note but from the word of God that confirmed and authenticated it as an answer from God to her doubts and anxieties.

There are many more such examples of this way in which Thérèse used and interpreted the Bible. What is evident in all of them is Thérèse's implicit conviction – affirmed by Vatican II in *Dei Verbum* – that, in and through the Scriptures, God speaks to us (cf. DV 25).

Thérèse had a deep conviction that the Scriptures were God's living and life-giving word, which was there for her benefit and at her service. And so, whenever she needed consolation or assurance in her trials and anxieties, or when she searched for confirmation of her teaching and mission, she went straight to the sacred text for light, guided by the Holy Spirit. And when she did so, she immediately alighted on the appropriate text for her particular predicament. The next example, as we shall now see, had a life-changing effect on Thérèse.

2. Discovering her Vocation and Mission

In Manuscript B, Thérèse tells how she was consumed with great desires and aspirations. She wished to unite every form of the Christian life in her own person, in order to glorify God. But she was only a human being, a nun enclosed in a cloister, which constricted and confined her universal desires for mission. She expresses her dilemma to Jesus in this way:

> To be Your *Spouse*, to be a *Carmelite*, and by my union with You to be the *Mother* of souls, should not this suffice me? And yet it is not so. No doubt, these three privileges sum up my true *vocation*: *Carmelite*, *Spouse*, *Mother*, and yet I feel within me other *vocations*. I feel the *vocation* of the WARRIOR, THE PRIEST, THE APOSTLE, THE DOCTOR, THE MARTYR. Finally, I feel the need and the desire of carrying out the most heroic deeds for *You*, *O Jesus*. I feel within my soul the courage of the *Crusader*, the *Papal Guard*, and I would want to die on the field of battle in defence of the Church. (SS, p. 192)

Thérèse immediately turns to Jesus, in faith, and asks: 'O Jesus, my Love, my Life, how can I combine these contrasts? How can I realise the desires of my poor *little soul*?' (SS, p. 192). She is confident that he has an answer and wishes to grant her desires.[6]

In characteristic fashion, she turns to the Scriptures for light. And she cries out: 'O my Jesus! what is your answer to all my follies?' (SS, p. 193). She then describes the way in which she began to obtain her answer:

During my meditation, my desires caused me a veritable martyrdom, and I opened the Epistles of St. Paul to find some kind of answer. Chapters 12 and 13 of the First Epistle to the Corinthians fell under my eyes. I read there, in the first of these chapters, that *all* cannot be apostles, prophets, doctors, etc., that the Church is composed of different members, and that the eye cannot be the hand at *one and the same time*. The answer was clear, but it did not fulfil my desires and gave me no peace. (SS, pp. 193-4)

At this point, Thérèse could appreciate the rationale of the answer provided, but she was not satisfied. She felt there *must* be another solution that would satisfy her desires. She continues:

Without becoming discouraged, I continued my reading, and this sentence consoled me: '*Yet strive after THE BETTER GIFTS, and I point out to you a yet more excellent way.*' And the Apostle explains how all *the most PERFECT gifts* are nothing without *LOVE. That Charity is the EXCELLENT WAY that leads most surely* to God.

I finally had rest. Considering the mystical body of the Church, I had not recognised myself in any of the members described by St. Paul, or rather I desired to see myself in them *all. Charity* gave me the key to my *vocation*. I understood that if the Church had a body composed of different members, the most necessary and most noble of all could not be lacking to it, and so I understood that the Church *had a Heart and that this Heart* was *BURNING WITH LOVE. I understood it was Love alone* that made the Church's members act, that if *Love* ever became extinct, apostles would not preach the Gospel and martyrs would not shed their blood. I understood that LOVE COMPRISED ALL VOCATIONS, THAT LOVE WAS EVERYTHING, THAT IT EMBRACED ALL TIMES AND PLACES... IN A WORD, THAT IT WAS ETERNAL!

Then, in the excess of my delirious joy, I cried out: O Jesus, my Love... my *vocation*, at last I have found it... MY VOCATION IS LOVE! (SS, p. 194)

Once again, we see the marvellous way in which Thérèse reads and interprets the word of God – a way that is prayerful, personal and existential. She penetrates, here, to the very heart of St Paul's teaching on love in the Body of Christ and appropriates it to herself, to the particular circumstance of her vocation. Through the illumination and inspiration of the Scriptures she comes to discover, understand, and assume more fully, her place and mission within the Church.

*

The Scriptures were of immense importance to Thérèse, a very great influence on her spiritual life and growth. They were the primary means of guidance and sustenance on her journey, framing and shaping her life.

Chapter Four

SPIRITUALITY OF
THE LITTLE WAY

Many people have heard of Thérèse's spirituality, often referred to as the 'Little Way'. But the very notion of a 'Little Way' gives rise to a number of questions: *Why* did Thérèse feel the need to discover an alternative spirituality? *What* led her to this course of action? *How* did she come to fashion her own Little Way? Was there not an *already existing spirituality* that appealed to her? We will now seek to answer these questions and to explain fully the Little Way of Thérèse.

I. Discovery of the Little Way

Towards the end of *Story of a Soul*, Thérèse recounts the experience which led to her discovery of her Little Way. She writes:

> You know, Mother, I have always wanted to be a saint. Alas! I have always noticed that when I compared myself to the saints, there is between them and me the same difference that exists between a mountain whose summit is lost in the clouds and the obscure grain of sand trampled underfoot by passers-by. Instead of becoming discouraged, I said to myself: God cannot inspire unrealisable desires. I can, then, in spite of my littleness, aspire to holiness. It is impossible for me to grow up, and so I must bear with myself such as I am with all my imperfections.

But I want to seek out a means of going to heaven by a little way, a way that is very straight, very short, and totally new.

We are living now in an age of inventions, and we no longer have to take the trouble of climbing stairs, for, in the homes of the rich, an elevator has replaced these very successfully. I wanted to find an elevator which would raise me to Jesus, for I am too small to climb the rough stairway of perfection. I searched, then, in the Scriptures for some sign of this elevator, the object of my desires, and I read these words coming from the mouth of Eternal Wisdom: *'Whoever is a LITTLE ONE, let him come to me.'* [Pr 9:4] And so I succeeded. I felt I had found what I was looking for. But wanting to know, O my God, what You would do to *the very little one* who answered Your call, I continued my search and this is what I discovered: *'As one whom a mother caresses, so will I comfort you; you shall be carried at the breasts, and upon the knees they shall caress you.'* [Is 66:13.12] Ah! never did words more tender and more melodious come to give joy to my soul. The elevator which must raise me to heaven is Your arms, O Jesus! And for this I had no need to grow up, but rather I had to remain *little* and become this more and more. (SS, pp. 207-8)

Here we can see the dynamics by which Thérèse came to fashion her Little Way. So important is this passage that it is worth considering it now in detail.

1. Desire for Holiness

Thérèse begins: 'You know, Mother, I have always wanted to be a saint' (SS, p. 207). Indeed, just before she entered Carmel at the age of 15, Thérèse wrote to Pauline: 'I want to be a saint' (LT 45). Evident from this is Thérèse's goal: *holiness*. Her desire 'to be a saint' was a constant ambition in her life, and we see it often in her writings, too. We will look at just two examples, drawn from different periods of her life.

In *Story of a Soul*, Thérèse recounts a grace she received sometime between the ages of ten and 13, when inspired by the zeal and glory of Joan of Arc. She writes:

> Then I received a grace which I have always looked upon as one of the greatest in my life because at that age I wasn't receiving the *lights* I'm now receiving when I am flooded with them. I considered that I was born for *glory* and when I searched out the means of attaining it, God inspired in me the sentiments I have just described. He made me understand my own *glory* would not be evident to the eyes of mortals, that it would consist in becoming a great *saint*! (SS, p. 72)

Much later, in her 'Act of Oblation to Merciful Love' – that solemn prayer of self-surrender to God – she sums it all up with this request to him: 'I desire, in a word, to be a saint' (SS, p. 276). From these two examples, ranging from childhood to maturity, it is clear that becoming a saint was not a mere fancy for Thérèse, but a continuous yearning.

2. Giving All

Granted that Thérèse desired to become a saint, how did she conceive of holiness? A clue is provided in a letter to Céline when Thérèse had just entered

Carmel: 'Jesus is asking ALL, ALL, ALL. As much as He can ask from the greatest Saints' (LT 57).[1] And about four months before her death, Thérèse wrote to Abbé Bellière: 'Dear little Brother, at the moment of appearing before God, I understand more than ever that there is only one thing necessary, that is, to work *solely* for *Him* and to do nothing for self or for creatures. Jesus wills to possess your heart completely [that is, 'ALL, ALL, ALL'], He wills you to be a great saint' (LT 244).

For Thérèse, then, holiness meant total availability to Jesus – it meant giving Jesus ALL. This desire is one of the principal elements of Thérèse's spirituality. It comes across strongly in a note to Pauline, in which she speaks about the desolation she has been experiencing during her Profession retreat and of the way in which she has been handling it:

> Today more than yesterday, if that were possible, I was deprived of all consolation. I thank Jesus, who finds this good for my soul, and that, perhaps if He were to console me, I would stop at this sweetness; but He wants that *all* be for *Himself*!... Well, then, *all* will be for Him, all, even when I feel I am able to offer nothing; so, just like this evening, I will give Him this nothing! (LT 76)[2]

Thérèse's Little Way, then, is not an end but a means. The means is *to give ALL to Jesus*, and the end is *holiness*.

3. An Impossible Goal

Thérèse continues: 'Alas! I have always noticed that when I compared myself to the saints, there is between them and me the same difference that exists between a mountain whose summit is lost in the clouds and the obscure grain of sand trampled underfoot by passers-by' (SS, p. 207). Here we see the real problem for Thérèse in her quest for holiness: she believes it to be an unattainable goal. She experiences herself as a 'grain of sand' who needs instead to become a 'mountain'. A sheer impossibility!

The underlying issue is that, together with her desire to become a saint, Thérèse is acutely aware of her own 'littleness' – her powerlessness, and inability to attain her goal. Feeling that she is not made of the stuff of saints, she soon realises that desires are not enough, her own efforts are insufficient, and that she cannot emulate or imitate the saints.

In making this comparison, Thérèse is thinking of the rigorous asceticism – the physical penances and mortifications – that the saints supposedly performed, in order to show their love for God and to give themselves to him. This model for becoming a saint was part and parcel of the religious ethos of the time, and it was the one proposed in the Lisieux Carmel.

It is important to note that Thérèse does not reject or condemn this conventional way of journeying to God. She is not even critical of it. She simply recognises that it is not for *her* to journey this way. She tried very hard – she tried her level best – to travel this way, but broke down under the demands; she simply could not manage to live up to this harsh regime.[3]

So, what is Thérèse going to do? Is she going to become discouraged and give up her desire for sanctity? NO! On the contrary: in the face of her desire for sanctity and her inability to attain to it by the conventional means, she reasons in this way: 'Instead of becoming discouraged, I said to myself: God cannot inspire unrealisable desires. I can, then, in spite of my littleness, aspire to holiness' (SS, p. 207). So, Thérèse has a deep conviction that her good desires, in this case her desire for sanctity, come from God and that God means to fulfil them – though not, of course, without her free cooperation.[4] This is how she acknowledges the fact that her desire for holiness is not doomed to futility.

Thérèse, then, is confident that God will find a *way* – a means proportioned to her nature – for her to attain her goal. She knows that God cannot ask of us what we do not have or cannot possibly give; he does not tease or torture us by inspiring unrealisable desires. For this reason, her 'littleness' cannot be an obstacle to holiness. She comments: 'It is impossible for me to grow up, and so I must bear with myself such as I am with all my imperfections' (SS, p. 207).

It is crucial to recognise that, in keeping with Thérèse's desire 'to give all' to Jesus, this is not a statement of complacency, but a deep cry from the heart. She has come to a deep realisation that she need not imitate the ways of the other saints but can accept herself as she is – little, weak, powerless – and begin from there her journey to holiness.

4. A Spiritual Elevator

Having accepted the reality of her situation, Thérèse decides to fashion her own way to the goal of holiness. She says: 'I want to seek out a means of going to heaven by a little way, a way that is very straight, very short, and totally new' (SS, p. 207). Here, Thérèse discloses the characteristics of her Little Way. It is:

'straight' – there are no bends in the road, no sharp turns, no possibility of getting lost; as such, it is the surest and least arduous way to one's goal;

'short' – it is the quickest way;

'new' – it has not been tried before; it is not in existence as far as she is aware.

Accordingly, Thérèse is going to be a trail-blazer ('new') who discovers the quickest ('short') and surest ('straight') way to her goal (heaven, or holiness).

Thérèse has now described her 'way' – but what is it going to be like in practice? As she ponders this, the image that comes into her mind is that of an elevator or lift – a new technological invention in her day, which she had experienced during a visit to Paris (cf. GC I, p. 306). The elevator fulfils exactly the characteristics she desires for her 'way': 'straight', 'short', 'new'! And so, she reflects: 'We are living now in an age of inventions, and we no longer have to take the trouble of climbing stairs, for, in the homes of the rich, an elevator has replaced these very successfully. I wanted to find an elevator which would raise me to Jesus, for I am too small to climb the rough stairway of perfection' (SS, p. 207). Thérèse wants her Little Way to be like the elevator: unlike the winding stairway, it can take one straight to the top and with minimum effort.

She then begins to search for the *spiritual* elevator that 'would raise me to Jesus'. As has already been seen, when Thérèse has a problem or seeks an answer to a difficulty, she immediately turns to the word of God for light. She recounts: 'I searched, then, in the Scriptures for some sign of this elevator, the object of my desires, and I read these words coming from the mouth of Eternal Wisdom: '*Whoever is a LITTLE*

ONE, *let him come to me.*' [Pr 9:4] And so I succeeded. I felt I had found what I was looking for' (SS, p. 208).

In these words from Proverbs, Thérèse recognised that it was she, the 'little one', who was being addressed; she felt herself called personally. As seen before, it is again clearly evident that Thérèse read the Scriptures in a personal, prayerful and existential manner – as a word at her service. However, she did not stop at this illumination; she was not satisfied, and she still needed to know what would happen if she responded to the call to come to Jesus. And so she continued reading: 'But wanting to know, O my God, what You would do to *the very little one* who answered Your call, I continued my search and this is what I discovered: "*As one whom a mother caresses, so will I comfort you; you shall be carried at the breasts, and upon the knees they shall caress you.*" [Is 66:13.12]' (SS, p. 208).

Finally, in this passage from Isaiah, Thérèse realised that if she responded to the call she would be raised to a profound intimacy with Jesus. He is the one who promises to raise the 'little one' who comes to him, like a mother who caresses her little child at her breast. 'Ah!' she exclaims, 'never did words more tender and more melodious come to give joy to my soul. The elevator which must raise me to heaven is Your arms, O Jesus!' (SS, p. 208). Here, then, is the answer: the *arms of Jesus* are to be her spiritual 'elevator' that will lift her to him. Thérèse exclaims: 'And for this I had no need to grow up, but rather I had to remain *little* and become this more and more' (SS, p. 208).

This is a magnificent discovery: her littleness, far from being an *obstacle* to holiness, is its *condition*! In other words, Thérèse acknowledges that if Jesus is to carry her, then she must have a *need* to be carried;

she must truly be a child who is too weak to walk by herself and so is totally dependent on him. After all, human parents do not carry their child once it becomes strong enough to walk by itself.

Therefore, in her quest for holiness, Thérèse comes to realise that she cannot become a saint – she cannot come to Jesus – all by herself. On the contrary, the way to attain this goal is to acknowledge her 'littleness' – her powerlessness, weakness and inability – and to become aware of it ever more acutely. And so, Jesus will come to carry her and bring her to himself. *Jesus* will make her a saint.

It must be noted here that this talk of 'remaining little' and 'becoming little more and more' may seem easy and simple to do. Yet, this is not so. As Thérèse will say in her letters, it is something people do not want to do. Why not? Because it is not easy truly to recognise and own the depths of our powerlessness, poverty, misery and dependence. The world puts pressure on us to grow up, to seek independence, to be in control of our life. This secular attitude can unwittingly slip into our relationship with God, too. This knowledge of our littleness and indigence is not arrived at by our own contrivance; it is a grace granted to those who truly strive 'to give all' to Jesus, and who in the process come to recognise their powerlessness and dependence.

5. Roots in the Old Testament

Here we have the account of *why* Thérèse sought for her own Little Way, and *how* she came to discover its roots in Scripture. But there is something intriguing here: while the Little Way is thoroughly in keeping with Jesus' teaching to his disciples, 'unless you change and become like little children, you will never enter the kingdom of heaven' (Mt 18:3), neither this gospel text nor the New Testament features in her search and exploration. On the contrary, she comes to her discovery from texts in the *Old* Testament: in Proverbs and Isaiah.

Added to this is an even greater surprise, one which shows the mysterious nature of divine providence. Thérèse did not have free access to the Old Testament; so how did she alight on these quotations? This is what happened: when Céline entered the Lisieux convent in 1894, she brought with her a small book in which she had copied out for herself her favourite Old Testament texts. When Céline entered Carmel, Thérèse used this book for her own meditation, and that is how she found the light and inspiration she needed when seeking and discovering her Little Way.

The vital text for Thérèse – '*Whoever is a LITTLE ONE, let him come to me*' (Pr 9:4; cf. SS, p. 208) – is the translation that Céline had copied out in her book. Modern translations, however, give: 'simple' (RSV) and 'ignorant' (JB); there is no mention of 'little one'. The version Céline worked from was inaccurate. Yet, it was precisely this mistranslation, 'little one', that resonated for Thérèse: she thought of herself primarily as a 'weak' and 'little' one, not a 'simple' and 'ignorant' one! So, had she had access to the accurate translation of this text, Thérèse would probably not have recognised herself addressed, and would not have found the light she was seeking. It is somewhat ironic that Thérèse, who was so particular about obtaining accurate translations of the Scriptures, and who wished to learn Hebrew and Greek in order to know the divine thinking exactly, discovered her Little Way to God through a faulty translation of the word of God!

This incident reveals how God's grace can come to us through any means he chooses. The impact of his message is not limited by human ways and means. As the saying goes, God can indeed write straight on crooked lines!

II. Defining the Little Way

Having seen why and how Thérèse came to her discovery, we can now begin to explore the spirituality of the Little Way. A good place to start is by examining this very title that Thérèse herself gave to her spirituality.

1. 'Little'

There are at least three reasons why the way of Thérèse is called 'Little':[5]

It is *simple*, in the sense that everyday life, with its humdrum character, is the place where this way to God is lived out. This is a spirituality that bypasses any esoteric, complex or extraordinary methods. We do not have to be clever or strong, removed from daily life, or able to perform any spectacular feats on our journey to God.

It conjures up the image of a *child*, aware of its littleness before God, and this powerfully expresses a person's eagerness to receive God's love.

It is a *short* way, removing any imagined distance between God and us. And, if followed seriously, it keeps us in close contact with our goal.

Very often, we imagine God as existing in some distant, celestial realm. For much of the time, we are able to live happily without reference to this God. However, in situations of difficulty, when life becomes unmanageable, we cry out to this God for assistance. In contrast, the spirituality of the Little Way, if lived conscientiously, keeps us in constant, habitual awareness of our need of God at all times, and of our total dependence on him.

2. 'Way'

Thérèse had no pretensions about her spirituality, which had been forged from her own experience of great desires coupled with humiliating failure and a sense of inadequacy. So, her spirituality is no more than *a* way – *her* way to God – which she suspects may also be helpful to many other little souls like herself.[6] As she said when Pauline asked her about the 'way' which she wished to teach souls: 'I want to teach them the little means that have so perfectly succeeded with me, to tell them there is only one thing to do here on earth: to cast at Jesus the flowers of little sacrifices, to take Him by caresses; this is the way I've taken Him, and it's for this that I shall be so well received' (LC, p. 257).

Although Thérèse had no exalted notions about her way, she had, nevertheless, a deep conviction that it somehow extended beyond herself, and that part of her mission from God was to make it known to his people. Accordingly, on July 17, 1897, she confided to Pauline: 'I feel that I'm about to enter into my rest. But I feel especially that my mission is about to begin, my mission of making God loved as I love Him, of giving

76

my little way to souls' (LC, p. 102). It was because of this mission that Thérèse now saw the importance of her manuscripts being published (cf. SS, p. xix).

Thérèse's certainty of the value and effectiveness of her Little Way for bringing spiritual profit to others is disclosed in this testimony from her novice, Sr Marie of the Trinity:

> On a certain occasion the Servant of God was speaking about the 'little spiritual way' she had taught me, and, just to test me, she said: 'When I am dead, and you no longer have anybody to encourage you to follow my "little way of trust and love" you'll probably abandon it, won't you?'
>
> 'Certainly not,' I answered. 'I believe in it so firmly that if the pope himself were to tell me that you had been wrong, I think I could still believe in it.'
>
> 'Oh! You should believe the pope before anybody else,' she replied sharply. 'But don't be afraid that he is going to tell you to change; I won't give him time to. If, when I get to heaven, I find that I have deceived you, I will obtain permission from God to come back straight away and tell you. Till then, believe that my way is safe and follow it faithfully.' (Test, pp. 233-4)

3. In a Nutshell

What, then, is Thérèse's Little Way? Pauline asked her this very question, and Thérèse answered: 'it's the way of spiritual childhood, it's the way of confidence and total abandon' (LC, p. 257). Pauline urged her to explain further what she meant by 'remaining a little child before God'. Thérèse replied:

It is to recognise our nothingness, to expect everything from God as a little child expects everything from its father; it is to be disquieted about nothing, and not to be set on gaining our living. Even among the poor, they give the child what is necessary, but as soon as he grows up, his father no longer wants to feed him and says: 'Work now, you can take care of yourself.'

It was so as not to hear this that I never wanted to grow up, feeling that I was incapable of making my living, the eternal life of heaven. I've always remained little, therefore, having no other occupation but to gather flowers, the flowers of love and sacrifice, and of offering them to God in order to please Him.

To be little is not attributing to oneself the virtues that one practises, believing oneself capable of anything, but to recognise that God places this treasure in the hands of His little child to be used when necessary; but it remains always God's treasure. Finally, it is not to become discouraged over one's faults, for children fall often, but they are too little to hurt themselves very much. (LC, pp. 138-9)

This response from Thérèse expresses her Little Way in a nutshell.

III. Living the Little Way

We have now reached the point where we can unpack the Little Way, so to speak, in order to draw out the dispositions for living it. They are not the only ones, but they are the main ones – and they are indispensable for following the spirituality of Thérèse.

1. Littleness and Humility

To have an attitude of littleness and humility is to recognise our weakness, powerlessness and inadequacy, which in turn leads us to acknowledge our total dependence on God – the fact that we need God's help to accomplish anything and everything. Thérèse says, moreover, that to acknowledge our littleness is to obtain God's powerful help. She writes to Céline: 'So let us line up humbly among the imperfect, let us esteem ourselves as *little souls* whom God must sustain at each moment. When He sees we are very much convinced of our nothingness, He extends His hand to us. If we still wish to attempt doing something *great* even under the pretext of zeal, Good Jesus leaves us all alone' (LT 243). In short, Thérèse is affirming that Jesus does not intervene where he sees us wanting to try and manage without him. However, as soon as he sees us struggling, he comes to our help. Thérèse continues: 'Yes, it suffices to humble oneself, to bear with one's imperfections. That is real sanctity! Let us take each other by the hand, dear little sister, and let us run to the last place… no one will come to dispute with us over it' (LT 243).

How many saints have had the audacity to affirm that humbly bearing with our imperfections is what constitutes true holiness? More commonly, it is associated with conquering our imperfections! But Thérèse puts the emphasis on the humble acceptance of our 'littleness'.

While this disposition is essential, it does not come easily to us. Thérèse writes to Céline: 'To be His, one must remain little, little like a drop of dew!... Oh! *how few* are the souls who aspire to remain little in

79

this way!' (LT 141). And writing to Abbé Bellière, she says that to enjoy the goodness and the merciful love of Jesus, 'one must humble oneself, recognise one's nothingness, and that is *what many souls do not want to do*' (LT 261).[7]

An attitude of littleness liberates people in their relationship with God, because it gives them rights as children which adults do not possess. A child is allowed to behave in ways that would not be acceptable or tolerated in an adult. A few weeks before her death, Thérèse said to Pauline:

> I will have the right of doing stupid things up until my death, if I am humble and if I remain little. Look at little children: they never stop breaking things, tearing things, falling down, and they do this even while loving their parents very, very much. When I fall in this way, it makes me realise my nothingness more, and I say to myself: What would I do, and what would I become, if I were to rely upon my own strength? (LC, p. 140)

2. Poverty

The disposition of poverty leads us to recognise that we own nothing, and to expect everything from God at every instant of our life. Thérèse confessed to one of her novices: 'I am very poor; it is the good Lord who provides me from moment to moment with the amount of help I need to practise virtue.'[8] Thérèse is happy to acknowledge her poverty because it is no obstacle to loving and serving God. She writes to Abbé Bellière: 'I hope, *Monsieur l'abbé,* that you will continue to pray for me who am not an angel as you appear to believe, but a poor little Carmelite, who is very imperfect and who in spite of her poverty has, like you, the desire to work for the glory of God' (LT 213).

Thérèse goes further. Not only is our poverty *not* an obstacle to a relationship with God, it actually gives us a hold on Jesus! To Céline, who felt discouraged and humiliated in the community because of her faults, Thérèse writes a note, using the persona of '*Mary, Queen of little* angels':

> If you want to bear in peace the trial of not pleasing yourself, you will give me a sweet home; true, you will suffer since you will be at the door of your house, but do not fear, the poorer you are the more Jesus will love you. He will go far, very far in search of you, if at times you wander off a little. He prefers to see you hitting against the stones in the night than walking in broad daylight on a path bedecked with flowers that could retard your progress. (LT 211)

This last statement is a strong affirmation that it is through our falls, imperfections and failings that we are kept humble, poor and dependent on Jesus. They are often the means by and through which grace comes to us. To live this poverty, however, is the difficulty, as Thérèse writes to her sister Marie:

> we must consent to remain always poor and without strength, and this is the difficulty, for: 'The truly poor in spirit, where do we find him? You must look for him from afar,' said the psalmist... He does not say that you must look for him among great souls, but 'from afar', that is to say in *lowliness*, in *nothingness*... Ah! let us remain then *very far* from all that sparkles, let us love our littleness, let us love

to feel nothing, then we shall be poor in spirit, and Jesus will come to look for us, and *however far* we may be, He will transform us in flames of love... (LT 197)

And a few weeks before her death, Thérèse tells Pauline how her own poverty has been a real source of grace to her:

I can depend on nothing, on no good works of my own in order to have confidence [that is, as she prepares to appear before the throne of judgment]. For example, I'd like to be able to say that I've carried out all my obligations of reciting my prayers for the dead. This poverty, however, was a real light and a grace for me. I was thinking that never in my life would I be able to pay my debts to God; this was real riches, real strength for me, if I wanted to take it in this way.

Then I made this prayer to God: O my God, I beg You, pay the debt that I have acquired with regard to the souls in purgatory, but do it as God, so that it be infinitely better than if I had said my Offices for the Dead... I felt this grace can't be expressed in words; it's far too sweet! We experience such great peace when we're totally poor, when we depend upon no one except God. (LC, p. 137)

In the last sentence, Thérèse affirms that true poverty brings a deep peace because it casts a person into the hands of God. Our peace is often disturbed because we withdraw from total dependence on God and place our trust in another person, or in ourselves, or in something other than God. However, because people are fragile, fallible, unstable, inevitably they cannot establish another person in peace. God alone can provide the security and assurance we seek.

3. Confidence

Confidence is the disposition that makes us bold enough to trust God, to approach him, and to seek his help on our journey to him. Confidence in God – to which are allied trust and abandonment – is the hallmark of Thérèse's spirituality of the Little Way. She writes, at the end of *Story of a Soul*: 'I go to [God] with confidence and love...' (SS, p. 259). And to Roulland she writes: 'my way is all confidence and love' (LT 226). Again, writing to her cousin, Marie Guérin, who was suffering from scruples and unsure whether to receive the Eucharist, Thérèse encourages her not to hesitate to do so, because: 'what offends [Jesus] and what wounds His Heart is the lack of confidence!' (LT 92). In other words: Jesus is hurt if we act as though his heart were not big enough, and full enough with love, to contain and embrace our miserable sins!

The basis of Thérèse's confidence in God was her understanding of God as *Merciful Love*. It is particularly this gospel understanding of God that is the foundation of her Little Way. This spirituality is pre-eminently biblical.

Thérèse's radical confidence in God's merciful love is strongly expressed in this bold statement – her very last – in *Story of a Soul*: 'Yes, I feel it; even though I had on my conscience all the sins that can be committed, I would go, my heart broken with sorrow, and throw myself into Jesus' arms, for I know how much He loves the prodigal child who returns to Him. It is not because God, in His anticipating Mercy, has preserved my soul from mortal sin that I go to Him with confidence and love...' (SS, p. 259; cf. LC, pp. 89 & 104). Thérèse does not qualify her statement of confidence in God's mercy. Even though she admits to a privilege – that of having been preserved from 'mortal sin' – she nevertheless does not look down in a condescending manner. Instead, she is filled with confidence in God's merciful love. Thérèse affirms that there is nothing we could possibly do that would prevent God from loving us and receiving us back into a relationship with him.

To Abbé Bellière who was dispirited about his faults and imperfections, Thérèse writes these words of consolation:

> [Jesus] has forgotten your infidelities now for a long time; only your desires for perfection are present to give joy to His Heart. I beg you, do not *drag* yourself any longer to *His feet*; follow that 'first impulse that draws you into His arms'. That is where your place is, and I have learned, more so than in your other letters, that you are *forbidden* to go to heaven by any other way except that of your poor little sister. (LT 261)

So, Thérèse assures the dejected young man that Jesus has no memory of past faults: that is, he does not keep a ledger of a sinner's failures! She urges Bellière to drop the 'heavy' load of past sins weighing him down and allowing him only to 'drag' himself to Jesus' feet. If he does so, he will be able to follow the desire of his heart and to leap into Jesus' arms.

Later on, in the same letter, Thérèse says: 'Ah! how little known are the *goodness*, the *merciful love* of Jesus, Brother!... It is true, to enjoy these treasures

84

one must humble oneself, recognise one's nothingness, and that is what many souls do not want to do; but, little Brother, this is not the way you act, so the way of simple and loving confidence is really made for you' (LT 261).

There are many other consoling passages in her writings on the merciful love of God – perhaps none more beautiful than these words to her sister Léonie, which illustrate well Thérèse's childlike confidence in God:

> I assure you that God is much better than you believe. He is content with a glance, a sigh of love... As for me, I find perfection very easy to practise because I have understood it is a matter of *taking hold of Jesus by His Heart...* Look at a little child who has just annoyed his mother by flying into a temper or by disobeying her. If he hides away in a corner in a sulky mood and if he cries in fear of being punished, his mamma will not pardon him, certainly, not his fault. But if he comes to her, holding out his little arms, smiling, and saying: 'Kiss me, I will not do it again', will his mother be able not to press him to her heart tenderly and forget his childish mischief?... However, she knows her dear little one *will do it again* on the next occasion, but this does not matter; if he takes her again *by her heart*, he will not be punished... (LT 191; cf. 258)

Here, Thérèse is inviting Léonie to have confidence that God is easily pleased by our tokens of love. And so she encourages Léonie to behave towards him like a child who is confident of its mother's love. This means recognising that nothing the child could possibly do will ever lead the mother to abandon it. In a certain sense, the mother is hostage to her child: it has only to turn to its mother with loving sorrow, and she is rendered powerless – won over by love for her child. To 'take Jesus by the heart', an expression of Thérèse, means precisely to be little and poor, confident in his merciful love – to trust and abandon ourselves to God, on our journey to him.

*

In exploring the Little Way, we have seen that the reason Thérèse set out to find her own way was because she wanted to become a saint. She desired a straight, short and new way, because she felt unable to travel the conventional way of the 'great' saints. Realising that she could not become a saint by her own efforts, she discovered that she had to become increasingly 'little', and so let Jesus carry her to himself. This is how, at the end of her life, Thérèse came to understand holiness, and it sums up well her Little Way to God:

> Sanctity does not consist in this or that practice; it consists in a disposition of heart which makes us humble and little in the arms of God, conscious of our weakness, and confident to the point of audacity in the goodness of our Father. (LC, p. 129)

For Thérèse, then, holiness depends on how we grow in our relationship with God, knowing ever more deeply our littleness and our need of his mercy. In this way, we are led to an authentic abandonment of ourselves to God, and willingly respond to his merciful love.

Chapter Five

PRAYER

A cursory reading of Thérèse's writings would suggest that she does not have much to say about prayer. And to a certain extent this is true. Unlike her spiritual parents, Teresa of Avila and John of the Cross, Thérèse did not set out intentionally to write a treatise on prayer or to communicate her spirituality. Her aim, in writing *Story of a Soul*, was simply to tell of her life with God, or as she herself puts it right at the beginning: 'I'm going to be doing only one thing: I shall begin to sing what I must sing eternally: *"The Mercies of the Lord"*' (SS, p. 13).

However, as Thérèse recounts her life with God, it becomes apparent that prayer is indeed an integral and essential part of it. As with all the saints, prayer was at the very core of Thérèse's life. Indeed, if prayer is understood as union and friendship with God, then her whole life was prayer. For Thérèse, prayer and life are of one piece – they are not two separate compartments but belong together.

I. Learning to Pray

Where and *how* did Thérèse learn to pray? From her own account, it is clear that she was nurtured in a prayerful environment. The Martin family were steeped in a faith which saw God in *all* the events of life. In this devout Christian home, prayer was part and parcel of the daily rhythm of life. This is how one author has described it:

> family prayers together, morning attendance at Mass, frequent reception of Holy Communion – rare in an epoch when Jansenism continued its ravages – Sunday Vespers, retreats. Their whole life revolved around the liturgical year, pilgrimages, a scrupulous regard for fasts and abstinences. Yet there was nothing stiff and bigoted in this family that was unacquainted with formality. They could be active and contemplative, feeding abandoned children, tramps, and the aged. Zélie took time out of her few short hours of nightly rest to attend to an ailing housemaid, while Louis went out of his way to help the disinherited, the epileptic, the dying. Both parents taught their children to respect the poor.[1]

Hence, her 'school of prayer', so to speak – the place where Thérèse first learnt of the Christian faith and the value of prayer – was her home and her family. *Story of a Soul* tells of some of the memories that deeply marked Thérèse and came to her mind as she looked back on her life.

Addressing Pauline, she recalls how this elder sister cared for her and taught her to pray after their mother's death: 'In the morning you used to come to me and ask me if I had raised my heart to God, and then you dressed me. While dressing me you spoke about Him and afterward we knelt down and said our prayers together' (SS, p. 36). This is but one random example of how she received her religious formation within the family home. There are many others in *Story of a Soul*.

Thérèse remembers especially the influence of her father, Louis, in teaching her to pray. She writes, for example:

Each afternoon I took a walk with Papa. We made our visit to the Blessed Sacrament together, going to a different church each day, and it was in this way we entered the Carmelite chapel for the first time. Papa showed me the choir grille and told me there were nuns behind it. I was far from thinking at that time that nine years later I would be in their midst! (SS, p. 36)

She also remembers the impact of attending Mass with her father:

When the preacher spoke about St. Teresa, Papa leaned over and whispered: 'Listen carefully, little Queen, he's talking about your Patroness.' I did listen carefully, but I looked more frequently at Papa than at the preacher, for his *handsome* face said so much to me! His eyes, at times, were filled with *tears* which he tried in vain to stop; he seemed no longer held by earth, so much did his soul love to lose itself in the eternal truths. (SS, p. 42)

Thérèse recalls, too, that she had only to look at her father at prayer 'to see how the saints pray' (SS, p. 43).[2] There is no doubt at all that Louis' prayerfulness was a deeply formative influence on the young Thérèse.

II. Temperament

While it is clear that Thérèse learnt the ways of prayer from her environment, she was also blessed with a prayerful and contemplative temperament; she was notably drawn to solitude and to love of nature, which is a quality shared by all of us to varying degrees. Here, then, are a few examples showing how Thérèse's prayer life was nurtured yet further.

1. Love of Solitude

Thérèse loved solitude – to be *alone* and to *ponder*. She had a deeply reflective temperament and attitude to life. Her aloneness, however, was not loneliness and introspection, but a communion with God, being present to him in simple faith. Recalling her fishing expeditions with her father at a very young age, Thérèse writes:

> They were beautiful days for me, those days when my 'dear King' took me fishing with him. I was very fond of the countryside, flowers, birds, etc. Sometimes I would try to fish with my little line, but I preferred to go *alone* and sit down on the grass bedecked with flowers, and then my thoughts became very profound indeed! Without knowing what it was to meditate, my soul was absorbed in real prayer. I listened to distant sounds, the murmuring of the wind, etc. At times, the indistinct notes of some military music reached me where I was, filling my heart with a sweet melancholy. Earth then seemed to be a place of exile and I could dream only of heaven. (SS, p. 37)

Thérèse also remembers how she unconsciously began mental prayer, at around the age of 11, just before her First Communion:

> At this time in my life nobody had ever taught me how to make mental prayer, and yet I had a great

desire to make it. Marie, finding me pious enough, allowed me to make only my vocal prayers. One day, one of my teachers at the Abbey asked me what I did on my free afternoons when I was alone. I told her I went behind my bed in an empty space which was there, and that it was easy to close myself in with my bedcurtain and that '*I thought*'. 'But what do you think about?' she asked. 'I think about God, about life, about ETERNITY... I *think*!' The good religious laughed heartily at me... I understand now that I was making mental prayer without knowing it and that God was already instructing me in secret. (SS, pp. 74-5)

2. Love of Nature

Thérèse was naturally awake to God's presence in the world, and especially in nature. The natural world was for her a means of prayer, of raising her soul to God and communing with him. She recalls her reaction to a storm that blew up while she was walking home with her father after one of their fishing trips:

> I remember one day when the beautiful blue sky became suddenly overcast and soon the thunder began to roll and the lightning to flash through the dark clouds. I saw it strike a short distance away, and, far from being frightened, I was thrilled with delight because God seemed to be so close! (SS, pp. 37-8)

When seeing the sea for the first time, she remembers:

> I was six or seven years old when Papa brought us to Trouville. Never will I forget the impression the sea made upon me; I couldn't take my eyes off it

since its majesty, the roaring of its waves, everything spoke to my soul of God's grandeur and power. (SS, p. 48)

On her trip to Italy, Thérèse was astounded by the beauty of God's creation. Not having travelled much until then, she had never dreamt that such beauty could exist on this earth. This is the impact it made on her:

Before reaching the 'Eternal City', the goal of our pilgrimage, we were given the opportunity of contemplating many marvels. First, there was Switzerland with its mountains whose summits were lost in the clouds, its graceful waterfalls gushing forth in a thousand different ways, its deep valleys literally covered with gigantic ferns and scarlet heather. Ah! Mother, how much good these beauties of nature, poured out *in such profusion*, did my soul. They raised it to heaven which was pleased to scatter such masterpieces on a place of exile destined to last only a day. I hadn't eyes enough to take in everything. Standing by the window I almost lost my breath; I would have liked to be on both sides of the car...

When I saw all these beauties very profound thoughts came to life in my soul. I seemed to understand already the grandeur of God and the marvels of heaven... I said to myself: When I am a prisoner in Carmel and trials come my way and I have only a tiny bit of the starry heavens to contemplate, I shall remember what my eyes have seen today. This thought will encourage me and I shall easily forget my own little interests, recalling the grandeur and power of God, this God whom I want to love alone. (SS, pp. 124-5)

The beauty and majesty of God's creation was for Thérèse a powerful stimulus to prayer and communion with God. But this communion was not for herself alone – it embraced others, too.

III. The Object of Prayer

For *whom* did Thérèse pray? Until the age of 14, her prayer was confined mainly to the needs and welfare of her family, relatives and friends. However, a significant turning-point occurred with the Christmas grace of 1886, which she refers to as 'the grace of leaving my childhood, in a word, the grace of my complete conversion' (SS, p. 98). This was a powerful influence in her life, and it occasioned a massive change in her. As Thérèse acknowledges: 'God was able in a very short time to extricate me from the very narrow circle in which I was turning without knowing how to come out' (SS, p. 101). The fruit of this grace was principally liberation from the hypersensitivity and self-preoccupation which had kept her locked up within herself and had, as she says, made her 'really unbearable' (SS, p. 97). There now came a certain expansion in Thérèse's horizons and vision, and an opening out to others: 'I felt *charity* enter into my soul, and the need to forget myself and to please others' (SS, p. 99). And she specifies: 'Jesus...made me a fisher of *souls*. I experienced a great desire to work for the conversion of sinners, a desire I hadn't felt so intensely before' (SS, p. 99).

From now on, Thérèse's prayer became more *universal* and ardently *apostolic*. One Sunday, looking at a picture of Jesus on the Cross, she was haunted by his cry, '*I thirst!*' (SS, p. 99), and she felt consumed with 'a *thirst for souls*', especially for those of '*great sinners*': 'I *burned* with the desire to snatch them from the eternal flames' (SS, p. 99). One famous example of this is her prayer for the repentance of the notorious murderer, Pranzini, who was condemned to death.[3]

As a result of her journey to Rome, the apostolic dimension of her prayer was further deepened and widened to include priests (cf. SS, p. 122). During this pilgrimage she had the opportunity, for the first time, of observing priests at close quarters. This experience surprised and even scandalised her. She confesses that until this journey she 'was not able to understand the principal aim of the Reform of Carmel' (SS, p. 122). The aim of Teresa of Avila, in her reform of the Order, was that the nuns were to be a powerhouse of prayer supporting the apostolate of all those who work for the welfare of the Church. Thérèse records her bewilderment: 'To pray for sinners attracted me, but to pray for the souls of priests whom I believed to be as pure as crystal seemed puzzling to me!' (SS, p. 122).

On this pilgrimage, Thérèse came to realise that 'though their dignity raises them above the angels, they are nevertheless weak and fragile men' (SS, p. 122). In short: priests, contrary to her previous beliefs and assumptions, had feet of clay and were sinners like the rest of humankind. This was a truly surprising discovery. Hence, she acknowledges that it was her journey to Rome that led her to understand more fully her vocation to Carmel. She said, when examined before her Profession: 'I came to save souls and especially to pray for priests' (SS, p. 149). The emphasis of Thérèse's prayer, then, shifted from praying exclusively for sinners to include praying for the spiritual welfare of priests.

IV. The Subject of Prayer

As with all who pray, Thérèse's prayer, and her *understanding* of prayer, also evolved over time. It can be said from the outset, however, that as Thérèse's intimacy with Jesus deepened, so her prayer became increasingly more *simple* – which does not mean more easy! On the contrary: as we shall see, prayer became more difficult – that is, less felt, less consoling. And this desolation came to a climax during the last 18 months of her life when she was deprived of *all* consolations and plunged into her 'night of faith'.

In Manuscript C, which contains Thérèse's most mature thoughts, she gives an extended treatment of the nature of prayer. She writes:

> How great is the power of *Prayer*! One could call it a Queen who has at each instant free access to the King and who is able to obtain whatever she asks. To be heard it is not necessary to read from a book some beautiful formula composed for the occasion. If this were the case, alas, I would have to be pitied! Outside the *Divine Office* which I am very unworthy to recite, I do not have the courage to force myself to search out *beautiful* prayers in books. There are so many of them it really gives me a headache! and each prayer is more *beautiful* than the others. I cannot recite them all and not knowing which to choose, I do like children who do not know how to read, I say very simply to God what I wish to say, without composing beautiful sentences, and He always understands me. For me, *prayer* is an aspiration of the heart, it is a simple glance directed to heaven, it is a cry of gratitude and love in the midst of trial as well as joy; finally, it is something

great, supernatural, which expands my soul and unites me to Jesus. (SS, p. 242)

By looking now more closely at each part of this statement, we will discover that it contains a complete account of Thérèse's understanding of prayer.

1. The Power of Prayer

Thérèse begins by acknowledging that prayer is powerful – that it has the capacity to bring about change. Using the analogy of chess, she compares prayer to the Queen, the most agile and powerful chess piece, the one that can most easily checkmate and capture the King. Behind this imagery is Thérèse's conviction that God (the King) is always susceptible and vulnerable to prayer (the Queen). Just as the King cannot refuse the Queen's request, God cannot resist the power of prayer, the pleas of those who turn to him.

Thérèse affirms that prayer and sacrifice are 'the invincible weapons which Jesus has given me. They can touch souls much better than words, as I have very frequently experienced' (SS, p. 241). There is a striking example of the power of prayer in the following incident. Thérèse relates how Sr Marie of the Trinity told her of a dream in which she believed God desired that her sister should also become a nun. Accordingly, the novice wished to write and inform her sister about this dream. However, she first needed the permission of the prioress as it was still Lent. Mother Marie de Gonzague refused her request, replying that 'it was not through letters Carmelites must save souls but through *prayer*' (SS, p. 241). When the disappointed novice reported back, Thérèse immediately responded: 'We must get to work; let's pray very much. What a joy if we are answered *at the end of Lent*!' (SS, p. 242). Sure enough, their prayer *was* answered! Thérèse exclaims: 'Oh! infinite mercy of the Lord, who really wants to answer the prayer of His little children. *At the end of Lent* one more soul was consecrated to Jesus. It was a real miracle, a miracle obtained by the fervour of a humble novice!' (SS, p. 242).

2. Vocal Prayer

For Thérèse, prayer is not necessarily tied to beautiful formulas read in books. It is important to note, though, that she does not reject vocal prayer – specially composed prayers found in books, or set prayers such as the 'Our Father' and 'Hail Mary'. Indeed, she affirms: 'I would not want you to believe, dear Mother, that I recite without devotion the prayers said in common in the choir or the hermitages. On the contrary, I love very much these prayers in common, for Jesus has promised *to be in the midst of those who gather together in His name*' (SS, p. 242). Thérèse also goes on to say that she found such prayers very helpful when it was difficult to recollect herself: 'Sometimes when my mind is in such a great aridity that it is impossible to draw forth one single thought to unite me with God, I *very slowly* recite an "Our Father" and then the angelic salutation; then these prayers give me great delight; they nourish my soul much more than if I had recited them precipitately a hundred times' (SS, p. 243).

Although Thérèse found set prayers helpful *in common* and during times of spiritual aridity, this was not her habitual way of praying: she found it hard to pray this way *privately*. The difficulty with vocal prayer was its repetitiveness. With respect to the rosary, for example, she humbly acknowledges what is a very common experience: 'when alone (I am ashamed to admit it) the recitation of the rosary is more difficult for me than the wearing of an instrument of penance. I feel I have said this so poorly! I force myself in vain to meditate on the mysteries of the rosary; I don't succeed in fixing my mind on them' (SS, p. 242).

The issue, here, is not that Thérèse fails to recognise the value of the rosary or does not want to pray it. On the contrary, she had a deep devotion to the Virgin Mary, and believed that the rosary was one of Mary's favoured prayers. So it was a bitter trial for Thérèse not to be able to pray the rosary well. She says: 'For a long time I was desolate about this lack of devotion that astonished me, for *I love* the Blessed Virgin so much that it should be easy for me to recite in her honour prayers which are so pleasing to her' (SS, pp. 242-3).

Thérèse would love to pray the rosary well, and is desolate at not succeeding. In spite of forcing herself, she fails; she finds that she cannot give her full attention to it or be nourished by it. So, what is her response going to be? And why? Thérèse continues to pray the rosary even though she *feels* she does it so poorly. She says: 'Now I am less desolate; I think that the Queen of heaven, since she is *my MOTHER*, must see my good will and she is satisfied with it' (SS, p. 243). Thérèse continues to pray the rosary, then, simply because she believes that it is pleasing to the Blessed Virgin and that Mary is aware of Thérèse's intention to do her very best to please her.

Thus, it is evident that Thérèse does not rely on her *feelings* in prayer. In other words, feelings do not determine *whether* she prays, or even *how* she prays. Implicit in her attitude and response here is an understanding of prayer as the expression of a *loving relationship.* As with any truly loving relationship, prayer involves self-giving which may at times be costly and burdensome. In praying the rosary, Thérèse does her best to show her love for the Blessed Virgin by giving of herself. So, for Thérèse, prayer is *primarily* about *self-giving.* As such, mere dissatisfaction or difficulty in prayer is not a reason to stop praying.

3. The Prayer of a Child

Prayer, for Thérèse, is uncontrived and unpretentious. Her way of praying is one of *childlike simplicity* and *spontaneity* – that is, she does not have to fashion her words carefully in order to attract God's attention or to persuade him to answer her. She just speaks with simple, loving faith to God who, she knows, *always understands* her. Implicit in this attitude is a key element of Thérèse's spirituality: that God is a Father who knows his children's needs and wishes. So Thérèse sees prayer as the simple turning of a child, with trust and confidence, to its Father, knowing that the Father will always listen, understand and respond.

4. An Affair of the Heart

In this important passage, Thérèse goes on to define prayer: 'For me, *prayer* is an aspiration of the heart, it is a simple glance directed to heaven, it is a cry of gratitude and love in the midst of trial as well as joy' (SS, p. 242).

Clearly, for Thérèse, prayer is *an affair of the heart.* In other words, prayer is *not primarily an activity*, even though prayer may involve such activities as saying the rosary, setting time aside, and meditating on the Scriptures. Rather, prayer is *a way of being with God*. As said earlier, for Thérèse, prayer and life are one. Prayer has to do with where our heart is at every moment of our life. It is a consciousness of the presence of God in *all* the events of our life, the trials as well as the joys. Prayer is a living in God, and a living of his life, with a deep sense of gratitude and love.

5. Union with Jesus

Finally, Thérèse affirms that prayer is 'something great, supernatural, which expands my soul and unites me to Jesus' (SS, p. 242). So, while we can dispose ourselves for prayer, and engage in this activity, prayer is essentially not our own achievement but a gift of God – 'supernatural', to quote Thérèse. And prayer can transform our life because it *expands our soul and unites us to Jesus*. According to Thérèse, then, true prayer affects our life and changes the one who prays by expanding that person's soul. In other words, prayer stretches us beyond our limits of loving, and, in so doing, transforms us ever more into the likeness of Jesus, by uniting us with him.

Towards the end of *Story of a Soul*, Thérèse sums up the nature of *her own prayer*. She quotes from the Song of Songs: 'Draw me, we shall run after you in the odour of your ointments' (Sg 1:3-4). These words express the substance of her prayer, which is about *her personal union with Jesus* and, through this union, the grace to draw others to him. Thérèse reveals that Jesus himself gave her an insight into these words from the Song of

Songs, as she was trying to work out how to pray for the many different intentions of those she loved:

> Since I have two brothers [Bellière and Roulland] and my little Sisters, the novices, if I wanted to ask for each soul what each one needed and go into detail about it, the days would not be long enough and I fear I would forget something important. For simple souls there must be no complicated ways; as I am of their number, one morning during my thanksgiving, Jesus gave me a simple means of accomplishing my mission.
>
> He made me understand these words of the Canticle of Canticles: '*DRAW ME, WE SHALL RUN after you in the odour of your ointments.*' (SS, p. 254)

Thérèse interprets this sentence as a plea 'to be united in an intimate way' (SS, p. 257) with Jesus, her Beloved. She declares: 'Dear Mother, this is my prayer. I ask Jesus to draw me into the flames of His love, to unite me so closely to Him that He live and act in me' (SS, p. 257). She believes that by uniting herself deeply with Jesus she will also bring all her loved ones to him. She writes:

> O Jesus, it is not even necessary to say: '*When drawing me, draw the souls whom I love!*' This simple statement: 'Draw me' suffices; I understand, Lord, that when a soul allows herself to be captivated by *the odour of your ointments*, she cannot run alone, all the souls whom she loves follow in her train; this is done without constraint, without effort, it is a natural consequence of her attraction for You. (SS, p. 254)

Thérèse realises that what we really desire for our loved ones is not just some *particular good thing*, such as good health, a good job and so on, but *the very best gift* they could have: namely, union with God. So, to pray for those we love is to desire that they be in communion with God. And Thérèse believes that the most effective way to achieve this is to be intimately united to God ourselves, by prayer. Then, those whom we hold in our hearts will also be drawn to God.[4] She says: 'I feel that the more the fire of love burns within my heart, the more I shall say: "*Draw me*", the more also the souls who will approach me..., the more these souls *will run swiftly in the odour of the ointments of their Beloved*, for a soul that is burning with love cannot remain inactive' (SS, p. 257).

Hence, for Thérèse, prayer is ultimately about union with Jesus. Prayer that is deep and personal will transform and unite us to Jesus; and it is *most effectively apostolic*: it brings other souls to Jesus.

V. Difficulties in Prayer

As for all who take prayer seriously, Thérèse, too, encountered difficulties in prayer, and we shall look at some of them now.

For most of her early years, however, right up to her entry into Carmel, Thérèse did not encounter any significant problems in prayer. On the contrary, she experienced great graces, delights and consolations – notable ones being, for example, her First Communion, her Confirmation, and the Christmas grace. At this time, Thérèse found prayer easy and consoling. In *Story of a Soul*, there is a certain poignancy when she looks back on her early years while now writing in an almost permanent state of spiritual aridity: 'how *light* and *transparent* the veil was that hid Jesus from our gaze!' she writes, referring to herself and Céline. 'Doubt was impossible, faith and hope were unnecessary, and *Love* made us find on earth the One whom we were seeking' (SS, p. 104).

With her entry into the convent, however, the consolations in prayer gradually diminished until she was eventually plunged into deep darkness and the 'night of faith', which was to last until her death. Thérèse's experience of prayer, then, became increasingly darker and more difficult, until she was left in a state of complete and total desolation. This is how she describes her 'night of faith':

> At this time I was enjoying such a living faith, such a clear *faith*, that the thought of heaven made up all my happiness, and I was unable to believe there were really impious people who had no faith... [Jesus] permitted my soul to be invaded by the thickest darkness, and that the thought of heaven, up until then so sweet to me, be no longer anything but the cause of struggle and torment. (SS, p. 211)

In this state, Thérèse confesses to her prioress:

> I must appear to you as a soul filled with consolations and one for whom the veil of faith is almost torn aside; and yet it is no longer a veil for me, it is a wall which reaches right up to the heavens and covers the starry firmament. When I sing of the happiness of heaven and of the eternal possession of God, I feel no joy in this, for I sing simply what I WANT TO BELIEVE. (SS, p. 214)

Generally speaking, it can be said that as Thérèse grew in intimacy with Jesus, her experience of prayer became increasingly difficult: arid, distracted, and more keenly dependent on a pure and naked faith, hope and love.

We can now look at some examples of Thérèse's difficulties in prayer and at how she coped with them.

1. Aridity and Desolation

Speaking about her Profession retreat, Thérèse makes this statement: 'it was far from bringing me any consolations since the most absolute aridity and almost total abandonment were my lot' (SS, p. 165). There was nothing particularly unique, however, about this retreat. *All* her retreats in Carmel, over her entire nine years there, were difficult: 'Just as all those that followed it, my Profession retreat was one of great aridity' (SS, p. 165). What is surprising and insightful is Thérèse's spiritual maturity, revealed in the way she interprets this experience. She says:

> Jesus was sleeping as usual in my little boat; ah! I see very well how rarely souls allow Him to sleep peacefully within them. Jesus is so fatigued with always having to take the initiative and to attend to others that He hastens to take advantage of the repose I offer to Him. He will undoubtedly awaken before my great eternal retreat, but instead of being troubled about it this only gives me extreme pleasure. (SS, p. 165)

Thérèse's interpretation is full of confidence in Jesus, and she abandons herself to him totally. She even attributes the cause of the aridity and desolation to

Jesus himself: that he is 'so fatigued' that he needs to rest. She is not unduly disturbed by the experience of desolation because she does not fear that Jesus has abandoned her. On the contrary, she accepts her experiences of desolation in serene and loving faith, and is happy to endure this for Jesus.

For Thérèse, then, we cannot have control of our prayer. It depends on Jesus and on what he does. If Jesus is, as it were, 'sleeping', then try as we might, nothing seems to happen. It is important to recognise that Thérèse is not devaluing arid states of prayer: she is simply affirming that she cannot manufacture her prayer by technique! And she understands that prayer should not be self-focused, or a seeking after consolations. On the contrary: prayer should be focused on what *we* can give to Jesus – namely, a place of hospitality, a place to rest.

These sentiments of abandonment and surrender to Jesus in faith and trust are accompanied by Thérèse's desire to give herself unreservedly to console Jesus. We can see this clearly in a letter to Pauline, written during Thérèse's retreat before Profession. She uses the metaphor of a journey to the summit of the '*mountain of Love*', to describe the way in which her Fiancé, Jesus, is leading her to himself:

> Before [Thérèse] left, her Fiancé seemed to ask her in what country she desired to travel, what route she desired to follow, etc., etc.… The little fiancée answered that she had but one desire, that of being taken to the summit of the *mountain of Love*. To reach it many routes were offered to her, and there were so many perfect ones that she saw she was incapable of choosing. Then she said to her divine

guide: 'You know where I want to go, You know *for whom* I want to climb the mountain, for whom I want to reach the goal. You know the one whom I love and the one whom I want to please solely; it is for Him alone that I am undertaking this journey. Lead me, then, by the paths which He loves to travel. I shall be at the height of my joy provided that He is pleased. Then Jesus took me by the hand, and He made me enter a subterranean passage where it is neither cold nor hot, where the sun does not shine, and in which the rain or the wind does not visit, a subterranean passage where I see nothing but a half-veiled light, the light which was diffused by the lowered eyes of my Fiancé's Face!...

My Fiancé says nothing to me, and I say nothing to Him either except that *I love Him more than myself*, and I feel at the bottom of my heart that it is true, for I am more His than my own!... I don't see that we are advancing towards the summit of the mountain since our journey is being made underground, but it seems to me that we are approaching it without knowing how. The route on which I am has no consolation for me, and nevertheless it brings me all consolations since Jesus is the one who chose it, and I want to console Him alone, alone!... (LT 110; cf. 111)[5]

It is clear from this extract that Thérèse's experience of prayer in Carmel was almost totally devoid of consolation; it was sustained only by a deep, dark and loving faith, trust and confidence in Jesus, and her utter abandonment of herself to him. It was the same even at the Eucharist, which was the centre of her life. Thérèse confesses: 'I can't say that I frequently received consolations when making my thanksgivings after

Mass; perhaps it is the time when I receive the least' (SS, p. 172). However, she goes on: 'I find this very understandable since I have offered myself to Jesus not as one desirous of her own consolation in His visit but simply to please Him who is giving Himself to me' (SS, p. 172). Once again, it is evident that Thérèse's whole attitude and perspective on prayer are primarily about *giving* to Jesus and not simply about *receiving*. And what Thérèse gives is her whole self – 'simply to please' Jesus.

The phrase 'to please Him' (SS, p. 172) is significant in Thérèse's writings. It governs her life and spirituality, which is about 'pleasing' Jesus and 'giving him everything'. So, for example, she writes to her sister Léonie:

> The only happiness on earth is to apply oneself in always finding delightful the lot Jesus is giving us. Your lot is so beautiful, dear little sister; if you want to be a saint, this will be easy for you since at the bottom of your heart the world is nothing to you. You can, then, like us, occupy yourself with 'the one thing necessary', that is to say: while you give yourself up devotedly to exterior works, your purpose is *simple*: to please Jesus, to unite yourself more intimately to Him. (LT 257)

2. Sleepiness and Distractions

Thérèse writes in *Story of a Soul* of how she thoroughly prepares her heart to receive Jesus in the Eucharist, and she says: 'It seems to me that when Jesus descends into my heart He is content to find Himself so well received and I, too, am content' (SS, p. 172). As always, Thérèse does her very best to give of herself in order to receive Jesus. But she immediately adds: 'All this, however, does not prevent both distractions and sleepiness from visiting me' (SS, pp. 172-3). Here, she is again acknowledging that she is simply not in control of her prayer. In spite of her best efforts, she cannot prevent being distracted and sleepy.

However, there is another side to this, too: Thérèse is also affirming that genuine prayer and communion with God are not impaired by distractions or sleepiness. And so, she acknowledges happily: 'at the end of the thanksgiving when I see that I've made it so badly I make a resolution to be thankful all through the rest of the day' (SS, p. 173). Hence, for Thérèse, prayer is a gift that we can only prepare humbly to receive; we cannot wilfully grasp it or manufacture it; we must leave it up to Jesus and then abide in peace.

This struggle with distractions, aridity and sleep was constant during most of Thérèse's life in Carmel. However, she never became discouraged by these trials. On the contrary: because of her genuine love for Jesus – that is, her desire to 'please' him and give him 'all' – she found ways to make the best of her spiritual afflictions and even to rejoice in them. This is what she says: 'Really, I am far from being a saint...; instead of rejoicing, for example, at my aridity, I should attribute it to my little fervour and lack of fidelity; I should be desolate for having slept (for seven years) during my hours of prayer and my *thanksgivings* after Holy Communion' (SS, p. 165). And then, almost with an air of reckless defiance: 'well, I am *not* desolate' (SS, p. 165).[6] Here we see Thérèse's realism and humility: she accepts the fact that she is not in control of her situation, but instead of becoming discouraged, she rejoices instead!

So, why is she 'not desolate'? This is how she interprets her struggles – full of hope and confidence in Jesus: 'I remember that *little children* are as pleasing to their parents when they are asleep...as when they are wide awake; I remember, too, that when they perform operations, doctors put their patients to sleep. Finally, I remember that: *"The Lord knows our weakness, that he is mindful that we are but dust and ashes"'* (SS, p. 165). Hence, Thérèse affirms that her sleep during prayer not only does not displease God, but while she is asleep he is not idle: he is delighting in his child and carrying out, in secret, his work of loving transformation in her. And so, she can boldly assert: 'You see, dear Mother, that I am far from being on the way of fear; I always find a way to be happy and to profit from my miseries; no doubt this does not displease Jesus since He seems to encourage me on this road' (SS, p. 173).

*

Thérèse's approach to her difficulties in prayer could at first sight be thought of as complacency. But that would be to misjudge her and to misunderstand her spirituality. Viewed in the context of her whole life which was characterised by a total giving of herself to Jesus, Thérèse's attitude is anything but indifference or complacency. What constitutes her practice and understanding of prayer is the wholeheartedness of her love, as seen in her desires and struggles – when she wishes simply to please Jesus and to give him all – together with her humble acceptance of her littleness, and her total confidence in God.

So, we might end with a short conversation, which Céline has recorded verbatim (LC, p. 228), when she found her sister awake one night in the infirmary with her hands joined together and her eyes looking up:

Céline: What are you doing? You should try to sleep.
Thérèse: I can't sleep, I'm suffering too much, so I am praying.
Céline: And what are you saying to Jesus?
Thérèse: I say nothing to Him, I love Him!

Chapter Six

THE MERCIFUL LOVE OF GOD

The merciful love of God is a central theme in the spirituality of Thérèse. In fact, it is *the* governing theme of her life and also the key to understanding her spirituality. We all view our own lives from a particular perspective – perhaps in the light of a calling or a close relationship. Thérèse interprets her own life primarily from the perspective of God's merciful love. In other words, that is the lens through which she views all the events of her life.

I. God's Merciful Love at work in the Life of Thérèse

1. God's Free Gift

At the very beginning of *Story of a Soul*, as we have seen, Thérèse outlines her aim in writing her autobiography: 'I'm going to be doing only one thing: I shall begin to sing what I must sing eternally: "*The Mercies of the Lord*"' (SS, p. 13). For Thérèse, then, her whole life is nothing other than a hymn to God's mercies.[1] She goes on to explain what she means by 'singing the mercies of the Lord': 'It is not, then, my life, properly so-called, that I am going to write; it is my *thoughts* on the graces God deigned to grant me' (SS, p. 15).[2] God's mercy is manifested in his graces – the ways in which Thérèse perceives God's presence at work in her life; the ways in which she experiences every aspect of her life as a gift from God, as God's loving kindness towards her. So, for example, she attributes to God's mercy the fact that:

- She was born into a particular family where she was surrounded with love and caresses (SS, pp. 15-17).
- She was blessed with a 'warm and affectionate' heart (SS, p. 17).
- She was granted a keen intelligence and memory (SS, pp. 16-17).
- She was protected from the dangers or seductions of the world (SS, pp. 83-4). With respect to this, she confesses: 'My heart, sensitive and affectionate as it was, would have easily surrendered had it found a heart capable of understanding it' (SS, p. 82). She also says that the fact that she was frequently misunderstood in her relationships was the work of Jesus protecting her from giving her heart away to creatures (SS, p. 83). Hence, she concludes: 'I have no merit at all, then, in not having given myself up to the love of creatures. I was preserved from it only through God's mercy!' (SS, p. 83).
- The prioress, Mother Marie de Gonzague, was strict and even harsh on her (SS, p. 150).
- Even the fact that she is scolded by a novice she attributes to God's mercy. Why? Because in this way God teaches her humility and gives her self-knowledge: 'Yes, it is the Lord who has commanded her to say all these things to me... This is the way God sees fit to take care of me... Ah! how great is His mercy; I shall be able to sing of it only in heaven' (SS, p. 245).

Hence, it is strongly evident that Thérèse understands her *whole* life and *all* the events in it as a mysterious unfolding of God's merciful love at work in her. It is important to note that, for Thérèse, God's gifts are not limited to the enjoyable and congenial happenings in her life: on the contrary, she sees God's presence in *everything* that happens to her, even the unpleasant events.

How did Thérèse feel that she came to be the recipient of this loving mercy of God? Did she earn it by good works? She would answer this with a categorical 'no': 'The flower about to tell her story rejoices at having to publish the totally gratuitous gifts of Jesus. She knows that nothing in herself was capable of attracting the divine glances, and His mercy alone brought about everything that is good in her' (SS, p. 15). Thérèse, then, is forthright in affirming that God's mercy is both the cause and the source of all that is good in her, and it is *unearned* and *unmerited*. In short, Thérèse acknowledges that God's merciful love is 'totally gratuitous' (SS, p. 15) – it is *sheer gift*.

2. The Need to be Little

However, Thérèse also maintains that, in bestowing his gifts, God has a *predilection*, a special love, for souls that are little, weak and poor. Littleness, weakness and poverty are the necessary dispositions in a soul for attracting God's loving mercy. One day, Thérèse received a letter from her sister Marie, despondent because, unlike Thérèse, she did not have a desire for martyrdom (cf. GC II, p. 997). This is Thérèse's reply: 'Ah! I really feel that it is not this [my desires for martyrdom] at all that pleases God in my little soul; what pleases Him is *that He sees me loving my littleness* and my *poverty, the blind hope that I have in His mercy...* That is my only treasure' (LT 197). And she continues:

> Oh, dear Sister, I beg you, understand your little girl, understand that to love Jesus, to be His *victim of love*, the weaker one is, without desires or virtues, the more suited one is for the workings of this consuming and transforming Love... The *desire* alone to be a victim suffices, but we must consent to remain always poor and without strength, and this is the difficulty... (LT 197)

This brings us back to the importance of recognising our own littleness. Our poverty and weakness, combined with a desire to love God, is the magnet that attracts God's loving mercy. Recounting how he has favoured her with many graces and brought her to Carmel, Thérèse reflects:

> When a gardener carefully tends a fruit he wants to ripen before its time, it's not to leave it hanging on a tree but to set it on his table. It was with such an intention that Jesus showered His graces so lavishly upon His little flower, He, who cried out in His mortal life: '*I thank thee, Father, that thou hast hidden these things from the wise and the prudent and revealed them to babes*', willed to have His mercy shine out in me. Because I was little and weak He lowered Himself to me, and He instructed me secretly in the *things* of His *love*. (SS, p. 105)

So God's merciful love shows itself in his bending down to those souls who are little, weak and poor, and raising them to himself. At the end of Manuscript

B, Thérèse exclaims: 'O Jesus! why can't I tell all *little souls* how unspeakable is Your condescension? I feel that if You found a soul weaker and littler than mine, which is impossible, You would be pleased to grant it still greater favours, provided it abandoned itself with total confidence to Your Infinite Mercy' (SS, p. 200).

Thérèse encountered this merciful God in her discovery of the Little Way.[3] Deeply conscious of her powerlessness, and searching for an 'elevator' that would raise her to Jesus, she came to realise: 'The elevator which must raise me to heaven is Your arms, O Jesus! And for this I had no need to grow up, but rather I had to remain *little* and become this more and more' (SS, p. 208). And she exclaims: 'O my God, You surpassed all my expectation. I want only to sing of Your mercies' (SS, p. 208).

Thérèse speaks of God's merciful love as being pent-up in his heart, and she sees that he longs for souls upon whom he can pour out this river of love. She cries out to him: 'It seems to me that if You were to find souls offering themselves as victims of holocaust to Your Love, You would consume them rapidly; it seems to me, too, that You would be happy not to hold back the waves of infinite tenderness within You' (SS, p. 181).[4] To this end, she offered herself as a victim to God's 'Merciful Love'.

Since God's mercy is drawn to the little, weak souls, Thérèse is insistent on remaining little and weak. In a letter to Abbé Bellière, she writes: 'Dear little Brother, I must admit that in your letter there is something that caused me some sorrow, and it is that you do not know me such as I am in reality... Oh, Brother! I beg you to believe me. God has not given you as a sister a *great* soul but a *very little* and a very imperfect one' (LT

224). And to prevent Bellière from thinking that she is just being modest, she immediately adds:

> Do not think that it is humility that prevents me from acknowledging the gifts of God. I know He has done great things in me, and I sing of this each day with joy... I am no longer disturbed at being a *little* soul; on the contrary, I take delight in this. That is why I dare to hope 'my exile will be short', but it is not because I am *prepared*. I feel that I shall never be prepared if the Lord does not see fit to transform me Himself. He can do so in one instant; after all the graces He has granted me, I still await this one from His infinite mercy. (LT 224)[5]

3. God's Own Choice

For Thérèse, God's merciful love is the guiding influence in her life. She sees that his loving mercy is supremely free, and she quotes the Letter to the Romans: 'God will have mercy on whom he will have mercy, and he will show pity to whom he will show pity. So then there is question not of him who wills nor of him who runs, but of God showing mercy' (SS, p. 13; cf. Rm 9:15-16). In other words, God is totally free as to how he bestows the graces of his mercy – it has nothing to do with our being worthy. To Bellière, who wishes to die a martyr, she quotes the same words of St Paul, to show him that even the grace of martyrdom is a gift of God's mercy (cf. LT 224).

It is in the light of God's sovereignly free and loving mercy that Thérèse interprets her own vocation: '[God] does not call those who are worthy but those whom He *pleases*' (SS, p. 13). What is implied here is that we might expect God to call those who are most worthy from a human point of view: the most devout, virtuous, clever, gifted, strong and so on. But God does not adopt human standards. His criteria are mysterious, precisely because he calls those 'whom He *pleases*'. Thérèse explains this in her letter to Bellière who, it appears, was entertaining lofty thoughts about her vocation as a Carmelite nun. She writes:

> It is true that to find great souls one must come to Carmel; just as in virgin forests there grow flowers of a fragrance and brilliance unknown to the world, so Jesus in His mercy has willed that among these flowers there should grow littler ones; never will I be able to thank Him enough, for it is thanks to this condescension that I, a poor flower without splendour, find myself in the same garden as the roses, my Sisters. (LT 224)

Here again, Thérèse is emphasising the fact that her vocation as a Carmelite is not the fruit of her own worthiness but an undeserved gift of God's mercy.

It is also through Thérèse's understanding of God's free mercy that she comes to understand why he appears to treat people differently – he even, we might say, seems to have preferences. In *Story of a Soul*, Thérèse confesses that she was surprised to see that God showered his favours on people who had offended him the most, like St Paul and St Augustine – men 'whom He forced, so to speak, to accept His graces' (SS, p. 14).[6] It was the same bewilderment when she read the lives of the saints: 'I was puzzled at seeing how Our Lord was pleased to caress certain ones from the cradle to the grave, allowing no obstacle in their way when coming to Him, helping them with such favours that they were unable to soil the immaculate beauty of their baptismal robe' (SS, p. 14). In fact, it seemed completely illogical: 'I wondered,' she continues, 'why poor savages died in great numbers without even having heard the name of God pronounced' (SS, p. 14).

4. A Gift for Each Person

As Thérèse looks back on her life, she reflects on how God has been active and present in it, and she comes to understand that God's merciful love is not only supremely free and unmerited, it is also *particular* and *personal*. She affirms that Jesus himself gave her an insight into this mystery by setting before her 'the book of nature' (SS, p. 14). There exist, she sees, many different kinds of flowers in the world of nature – lilies, roses, daisies, violets and so on – each one beautiful *in its own way* and giving pleasure to the eye precisely *because of their difference*. So, too, the world of souls, which is 'Jesus' garden' (SS, p. 14), contains a wide variety of souls and they 'give joy to God's glances' (SS, p. 14). What is important, says Thérèse, is that each soul, like each kind of flower, be exactly what it is and not try to be what it is not.[7]

Thérèse continues: 'I understood, too, that Our Lord's love is revealed as perfectly in the most simple soul who resists His grace in nothing as in the most excellent soul' (SS, p. 14). She then proceeds to make an audacious statement about the humility of love: 'since the nature of love is to humble oneself, if all souls resembled those of the holy Doctors who illumined the Church with the clarity of their teachings, it seems God would not descend so low when coming to their heart' (SS, p. 14). That is to say: if all souls were spiritual or intellectual giants, then God would not have to exercise his mercy to the same great extent! She writes:

> But He created the child who knows only how to make his feeble cries heard; He has created the poor savage who has nothing but the natural law to guide him. It is to their hearts that God deigns to lower Himself. These are the wild flowers whose simplicity attracts Him. When coming down in this way, God manifests His infinite grandeur. Just as the sun shines simultaneously on the tall cedars and on each little flower as though it were alone on the earth, so Our Lord is occupied particularly with each soul as though there were no others like it. And just as in nature all the seasons are arranged in such a way as to make the humblest daisy bloom on a set day, in the same way, everything works out for the good of each soul. (SS, pp. 14-15)

So, God's merciful love accommodates itself to us according to our individual nature and circumstances. His grace is at work in a particular and personal way in the life of each of us individually – for our own good, and to bring us to salvation.

II. God's Mercy or God's Justice?

People often ask: How can we reconcile God's *mercy* with God's *justice*? Thérèse broaches this problem towards the end of Manuscript A:

> O my dear Mother! after so many graces can I not sing with the Psalmist: '*How GOOD is the Lord, his MERCY endures forever!*' [Ps 117:1] It seems to me that if all creatures had received the same graces

I received, God would be feared by none but would be loved to the point of folly; and through *love*, not through fear, no one would ever consent to cause Him any pain. I understand, however, that all souls cannot be the same, that it is necessary there be different types in order to honour each of God's perfections in a particular way. To me He has granted His *infinite Mercy*, and *through it* I contemplate and adore the other divine perfections! All of these perfections appear to be resplendent *with love*; even His Justice (and perhaps this even more so than the others) seems to me clothed in *love*. What a sweet joy it is to think that God is *Just*, i.e., that He takes into account our weakness, that He is perfectly aware of our fragile nature. What should I fear then? Ah! must not the infinitely just God, who deigns to pardon the faults of the prodigal son with so much kindness, be just also toward me who 'am with Him always'? (SS, p. 180)

How Thérèse understands the dilemma of God's mercy and justice will be explored by looking more closely at this important passage.

1. A God of Mercy

Looking back on all the gifts of God that have brought her to Carmel, Thérèse exclaims: 'O my dear Mother! after so many graces can I not sing with the Psalmist: "*How GOOD is the Lord, his MERCY endures forever!*"' (SS, p. 180). She then reflects: 'It seems to me that if all creatures had received the same graces I received, God would be feared by none but would be loved to the point of folly; and through *love*, not through fear, no one would ever consent to cause Him any pain' (SS, p. 180).

120

Behind this talk of 'love' and 'fear' of God, Thérèse is exposing the religious climate of her time. The predominant religious ethos was Jansenism, which tended to focus on God's justice, to the virtual neglect of his mercy. Accordingly, the primary image of the Jansenists' God was that of a tyrant exacting strict justice, and such a God expected his people to keep his laws and commandments without any mitigation. This image of a demanding God became an oppressive and crippling figure for people and bred a relationship based on *fear*. They felt themselves constantly threatened by eternal damnation, for the slightest breaches of the law. A relationship with God built on fear contributes greatly to the flourishing of scruples, from which Thérèse herself suffered in her earlier years. The tragedy of this is that while people could still have a certain relationship with God, they could hardly *love* such a God. So, we find people trying to do the right thing and avoid sin, not because they loved God but because they feared punishment. To put it another way: they attempted to get into heaven not by the front door through active love, but through the back door by not doing anything wrong.

Thérèse continues: 'I understand, however, that all souls cannot be the same, that it is necessary there be different types in order to honour each of God's perfections in a particular way. To me He has granted His *infinite Mercy*, and *through it* I contemplate and adore the other divine perfections!' (SS, p. 180). It is significant that Thérèse does not stop to be critical of the Jansenistic image of God. Nowhere does she directly attack or condemn this image. On the contrary, she acknowledges that there are many perfections in God, all of which must be highlighted and honoured.

Nonetheless – in a way that was unusual and bold for her time – Thérèse simply refused to believe in such a God. She says that she views *all* the perfections of God – including his justice – through the lens of his mercy. Consequently, her image of God is thoroughly evangelical; it is based on the Gospels, which portray a God of extravagant mercy (cf. Lk 15:1-32). We can see how this perspective must have been an eye-opener! Bellière, for example, writes to Thérèse:

> Do you realise you are opening up new horizons for me? In your last letter especially, I find some insights on the mercy of Jesus, on the familiarity He encourages, on the simplicity of the soul's relations with this great God which had little touched me until the present because undoubtedly it had not been presented to me with this simplicity and unction your heart pours forth. (GC II, pp. 1143-4)

A week later, when the lesson has sunk in even more deeply, Bellière writes again, contrasting the image of God that Thérèse presents to him with the Jansenistic image that was commonly preached and accepted. And interestingly, he notes how these two images affect his own relationship with God:

> If I was shown an angered God, His hand always armed to strike, I became discouraged, I did nothing. But if I see Jesus waiting patiently my return to Him, granting me a new grace after I have asked pardon for a new sin, I am conquered, and I climb again into the saddle. (GC II, p. 1158)

Bellière is acknowledging that human beings cannot stand face to face with a God of exacting justice. We become discouraged. Hence, to attempt to do so is to be defeated from the start. However, to recognise that God is merciful empowers us to rise from failure and try again.

2. The Joy of God's Justice

In her important passage from Manuscript A, Thérèse continues: 'All of these perfections appear to be resplendent *with love*; even His Justice (and perhaps this even more so than the others) seems to me clothed in *love*. What a sweet joy it is to think that God is *Just*, i.e., that He takes into account our weakness, that He is perfectly aware of our fragile nature' (SS, p. 180).

These words – 'What a sweet joy it is to think that God is *Just*' – are truly surprising and radical! Here, at a time that was rife with Jansenism, Thérèse announces that God's divine justice – the attribute of God that was most feared – is something that, far from fearing, she actually rejoices in!

The Jansenists feared the justice of God, precisely because they had polarised God's attributes of justice and mercy – they saw them as opposites. Consequently, they misunderstood the nature of divine justice. Thérèse, however, does *not* separate these two perfections in God. She holds both of them in a balanced and creative tension, and so is able to reinterpret the nature of divine justice. Accordingly, for Thérèse, there is no conflict between God's justice and mercy. On the contrary, she is grateful that God is just – because, as she says, 'He takes into account our weakness' (SS, p. 180). Therefore we have nothing to fear. She points out that because God is merciful he is truly just, and because God is just he is truly merciful.

The fact that God, in his justice, takes account of our 'fragile nature' (SS, p. 180) is illustrated further when we read a letter from Thérèse to Fr Roulland. This priest was a missionary in China, and in real danger of being killed by bandits. He writes to Thérèse, explaining his precarious situation: 'If the bandits kill me, and if I am not worthy to enter heaven immediately, you will draw me out of purgatory, and I shall go to await you in paradise' (GC II, p. 1063). In her reply, Thérèse reacts strongly to Roulland's statement, which she sees as manifesting a fear of God's justice and therefore a lack of confidence in God's mercy. She writes:

I do not understand, Brother, how you seem to doubt your immediate entrance into heaven if the infidels were to take your life. I know one must be very pure to appear before the God of all Holiness, but I know, too, that the Lord is infinitely just; and it is this justice which frightens so many souls that is the object of my joy and confidence. To be just is not only to exercise severity in order to punish the guilty; it is also to recognise right intentions and to reward virtue. I expect as much from God's justice as from His mercy. It is because He is just that 'He is compassionate and filled with gentleness, slow to punish, and abundant in mercy, for He knows our frailty, He remembers we are only dust. As a father has tenderness for his children, so the Lord has compassion on us!!' (LT 226; cf. Ps 102:8.14.13)

3. The Heart of God

For Thérèse, the knowledge and acceptance of God's loving mercy gives us a new and fresh start; it also makes us daring in our relationship with God because it gives hope and expels fear from our life. Sr Marie of the Trinity gave the following testimony to the diocesan tribunal:

> Sister Thérèse had made her own that saying of St John of the Cross: 'One obtains from God what one hopes for.' It was a saying she often repeated to me. I once asked her if our Lord was displeased with me, seeing I was so imperfect. 'Rest assured,' she said, 'that he whom you have taken as your spouse has all the perfections that one could desire, but, if I may say so, he has one great weakness: he is blind! And there is one branch of knowledge he is ignorant of – mathematics. If he were able to see clearly and keep proper accounts, the sight of our sins would make him annihilate us. But no, his love for us makes him positively blind! Look at it this way. If the greatest sinner on earth repented of all his offences at the last moment and died in an act of love, God would not stop to weigh up the numerous graces which the unfortunate man had wasted and the crimes he had been guilty of; he counts only that last prayer and receives him into the arms of his mercy without delay. (Test, p. 233)

So, God's loving mercy gives hope because he does not bestow his merciful love by measure. God does not tally or weigh up our sins when pouring his mercy on us. He loves without calculation.

Again, when Bellière is dispirited about how poorly he has served God and wasted his earlier years (cf. GC II, p. 1125), Thérèse replies:

> Do not think you frighten me by speaking 'about your beautiful, wasted years'. I myself thank Jesus, who has looked at you with a *look of love* as, in the

past, He looked at the young man in the Gospel. More blessed than he, you have answered faithfully the Master's call, you have left all to follow Him, and this at the *most beautiful age* of your life, at eighteen. Ah! Brother, like me you can sing the mercies of the Lord, they sparkle in you in all their splendour. (LT 247)

In other words, we can either, like Abbé Bellière, get discouraged about our lives, seeing only our failures in loving God; or, like Thérèse, we can see our lives as a work of God's loving mercy bringing us to the present point where we can respond more fully to God. And this is the difference: Bellière looks primarily at what *he has done* – his own efforts in journeying to God; while Thérèse looks at what *God has been doing* – his loving mercy leading Bellière to himself. Thérèse continues:

You love St. Augustine, Saint Magdalene, these souls to whom 'many sins were forgiven because they loved much'. I love them too, I love their repentance, and especially...their loving audacity! When I see Magdalene walking up before the many guests, washing with her tears the feet of her adored Master, whom she is touching for the first time, I feel that *her heart* has understood the abysses of love and mercy *of the Heart of Jesus*, and, sinner though she is, this Heart of love was not only disposed to pardon her but to lavish on her the blessings of His divine intimacy, to lift her to the highest summits of contemplation. (LT 247)

So Thérèse urges Bellière to take heart from the example of Mary Magdalene. This woman from the Gospels was able to be so daring and bold with Jesus, to walk up to him in front of so many people and wash his feet with tears, because she knew in her own heart that Jesus' heart was full of merciful love. In short, Mary Magdalene did not look at herself – if she had done, she would not have dared to go to Jesus. Rather, she looked at Jesus and recognised his loving mercy towards her. And this enabled her to make contact with him and to experience the blessings of his loving mercy, which was to raise her up to intimacy with himself.

4. Confidence in God's Mercy

Thérèse continues to Bellière: 'Ah! dear little Brother, ever since I have been given the grace to understand also the love of the Heart of Jesus, I admit that it has expelled all fear from my heart. The remembrance of my faults humbles me, draws me never to depend on my strength which is only weakness, but this remembrance speaks to me of mercy and love even more' (LT 247). Again, unlike Bellière, who becomes despondent when he thinks of his past, Thérèse, conscious of God's merciful love, can reflect on her own past without becoming sad or fearful. The remembrance of her faults serves only to make her recognise more acutely her absolute need for God; and it uncovers, even more vividly and powerfully, the depths of God's merciful love towards her.

With this deep experience of God's merciful love, and her confidence in his mercy, Thérèse feels herself to be in solidarity with sinners. She wishes to become an apostle of mercy to them – to proclaim his mercy to *all*, especially to those bereft of hope and who most need to hear this truth, this good news. Hence, we have this beautiful testimony from Sr Marie of the Trinity: '[Thérèse] once confided to me: "If I had not been accepted in Carmel I would have entered a Refuge [an institution for reformed prostitutes] and lived out my days there, unknown and despised among the poor penitents. I would have been happy to be taken for one of them, and would have become an apostle among them, telling them what I thought of God's mercy"' (Test, p. 248).

*

God's merciful love is at the very heart of Thérèse's spirituality. Indeed, if Thérèse had had to answer the question, 'Who is God?', she would have replied: 'He is Merciful Love.' God's mercy is the unmerited, sovereignly free kindness of God, bestowing itself on those poor, little, weak and struggling souls who desire intimacy with him. This emphasis on God's merciful love for all his children was, and still is today, Thérèse's principal message for the Church.[8] Her conviction that God *is* Merciful Love is what empowers Thérèse to journey to God with confidence, no matter in what condition she may find herself. It is her final word – for this is how her autobiography concludes:

> Yes, I feel it; even though I had on my conscience all the sins that can be committed, I would go, my heart broken with sorrow, and throw myself into Jesus' arms, for I know how much He loves the prodigal child who returns to Him. It is not because God, in His anticipating Mercy, has preserved my soul from mortal sin that I go to Him with confidence and love... (SS, p. 259)

Chapter Seven

TRUTH

It is an interesting fact that in the major world religions God is associated, and even identified, with Truth. In the Christian gospel, for example, Jesus defines himself as 'the Way, the Truth and the Life' (Jn 14:6). The devout Hindu political and religious leader, Mahatma Gandhi, affirms: 'Truth is the supreme God for me. Truth is God... There is no other god than Truth.'[1] And we can also quote Edith Stein, the Carmelite saint who was Jewish by birth: 'It has always been far from me to think that God's mercy allows itself to be circumscribed by the visible church's boundaries. God is truth. All who seek truth seek God, whether this is clear to them or not.'[2] Hence, the one who seeks truth is also seeking God.

I. Truth in Thérèse's Life

Truth is one of the major themes in Thérèse's life and spirituality. The search for truth, and the desire to live in the truth, was an integral part of her whole life.

From her earliest years, Thérèse could not abide lies, or situations of ambiguity, characterised by duplicity or falseness. As a young child, for example, if Thérèse believed she had done something wrong, she felt an immediate and pressing need to disclose it, to confess her fault and to obtain forgiveness. In short, the truth of her situation had to be revealed; there was no hiding from the truth. For Thérèse, to manifest the truth of her situation removed the ambiguity in which she found herself and restored her security and peace of mind. Her mother testifies to this trait of Thérèse in a letter to Pauline: 'she has a heart of gold; she is very lovable and frank; it's curious to see her running after me making her confession: "Mama, I pushed Céline once, I hit her once, but I won't do it again." (It's like this for everything she does.)' (SS, p. 22). Or again, Zélie reports:

> She becomes emotional very easily. As soon as she does anything wrong, everybody must know it. Yesterday, not meaning to do so, she tore off a small piece of wallpaper. She wanted to tell her Father immediately, and you would have pitied her to see her anxiety. When he returned four hours later and everybody had forgotten about it, she ran at once to Marie, saying: 'Marie, hurry and tell Papa I tore the paper.' Then she awaited her sentence as if she were a criminal. There is an idea in her little head that if she owns up to something, she will be more readily forgiven. (SS, pp. 18-19)

Although everyone had forgotten about the incident, Thérèse could not rest until the truth was revealed. For Thérèse, then, truth meant being transparent in her conduct. This was important to her: she did not want to have guilty secrets or engage in surreptitious behaviour.[3]

This transparency was so deeply rooted in Thérèse's life that she had a repugnance for any kind of 'pretence'. A few months before her death, when Pauline asked her 'to say a few edifying...words to Dr. de Cornière', Thérèse replied: 'Ah! little Mother, this isn't my little style. Let Doctor de Cornière think what he wants. I love only simplicity; I have a horror for "pretence". I assure you that to do what you want would be bad on my part' (LC, p. 77). On another occassion, Pauline felt that Thérèse was downhearted in spite of her happy mood, and she said: 'It's for our sake that you take on this happy mood and say these cheerful things, isn't it?' To which Thérèse replied: 'I always act without any "pretence"' (LC, p. 92; cf. pp. 83 & 146).

Hence, for Thérèse, the truth as lived in our relationship with others has to do with simplicity and authenticity. We must simply be what we are, here and now as God wishes us to be, and not put on a front in order to deceive ourselves or others. She did not soften uncomfortable situations, which could run the risk of misleading people.

II. Truth and Charity

The authenticity of Thérèse is the fruit of living in the truth. But while it involves simple directness in one's conduct and relationships, it is not a self-assertion that neglects other people's feelings! Nor is it a self-projection that does not consider the consequences of our words and deeds for others, such as the attitude, 'This is the way I am: like it or lump it!'

Thérèse recounts how she coped with the natural antipathy she felt towards one of the nuns in community. She admits, in *Story of a Soul*: '[this Sister] has the faculty of displeasing me in everything, in her ways, her words, her character, everything seems *very disagreeable* to me' (SS, p. 222). So Thérèse made doubly sure to make her behaviour charitable: 'I took care to render her all the services possible, and when

I was tempted to answer her back in a disagreeable manner, I was content with giving her my most friendly smile, and with changing the subject of the conversation' (SS, pp. 222-3).

We might ask this question: Was Thérèse not being insincere and untruthful? Was she not contradicting her horror of 'pretence'? It might well seem, at first sight, to be the case. But, Thérèse would say: 'No' – she would insist that there was no 'pretence' or untruthfulness in her relationship with this nun. Why? Because, for Thérèse, authenticity is rooted, not in self-assertion or self-centredness but in charity and self-giving. In short: for Thérèse, the virtue of living in the truth is not independent of, but related to, living in charity.

In this respect, Thérèse might say that truth without charity is a vice and not a virtue. Hence, she was careful how she used it. She tried not to use the truth to hurt others, as we see from the following incident recorded by Pauline: 'Sister St. Stanislaus, the main infirmarian, had left Sister Thérèse by herself all through Vespers, forgetting to close the infirmary door and window; there was a very strong draught, as a consequence, and Mother Prioress demanded an explanation when she found her in this condition'. Thérèse confided to Pauline: 'I told Mother Prioress the truth, but while I was speaking, there came to my mind a more charitable way of expressing it than the one I was going to use, and still it wasn't wrong, certainly. I followed my inspiration, and God rewarded me for it with a great interior peace' (LC, p. 138).

As Thérèse sees: truth, in our relationship with others, does not consist only in *what* we say, but also in *how* we say it. This is an echo of St Paul's words to the Ephesians, when he urges them *to speak the truth* (to one another) *in love* (cf. Eph 4:15).

This relationship between truth and charity was central to Thérèse's life. For Thérèse, love is founded on truth and cannot exist in situations of false compromise or deception; examples would be circumstances of fearing to speak, or live, the truth; of trying to manipulate, dominate and control others; or of currying favour with others. For Thérèse, truth is a sacred trust; it is a responsibility we have, in loving others and caring for them. This fact impressed itself on Thérèse from her childhood. She remembers:

I was still very little when Aunt gave me a story to read that surprised me very much. I saw where they were praising a boarding school teacher because she was able to extricate herself cleverly from certain situations without offending anyone. I took note above all of this statement: 'She said to this one: You're not wrong; to that one: You are right.' And I thought to myself: This is not good! This teacher should have had no fear and should have told her little girls that they were wrong when this was the truth.

And even now I haven't changed my opinion. I've had a lot of trouble over it, I admit, for it's always so easy to place the blame on the absent, and this immediately calms the one who is complaining. Yes, but... it is just the contrary with me. If I'm not loved, that's just too bad! I tell the whole truth, and if anyone doesn't wish to know the truth, let her not come looking for me. (LC, p. 38)

Thérèse confesses that she is no diplomat when it comes to speaking the truth. She will not engage in a false compromise where the truth is concerned, because to do so would not be an act of true loving.

In *Story of a Soul*, Thérèse recounts a personal incident which shows how she lived this responsibility of truth in her loving care for others. In the novitiate she was assigned a spiritual companion, Sr Martha of Jesus, eight years her senior. This companionship was intended as a means to foster mutual spiritual growth. In other words, each was to support the other to grow in grace and virtue. Thérèse noticed that Sr Martha had certain faults, among which was her strong and disordered attachment to Mother Marie de Gonzague. After trying unsuccessfully to alert her to this gently, Thérèse says: 'I was thinking regretfully that our conversations were not attaining their desired purpose. God made me feel that the moment had come and I must no longer fear to speak out or else end these interviews which resembled those of two worldly friends' (SS, p. 236).

Out of her responsibility and care for her companion, Thérèse decided to speak the whole truth as she saw it. This is how she describes her conduct. Placing Sr Martha's head upon her heart:

I...told her with tears in my voice *everything I was thinking about her*, but I did this with such tender expressions and showed her such a great affection that very soon her tears were mingled with mine. She acknowledged with great humility that what I was saying was true, and she promised to commence a new life, asking me as a favour always to let her know her faults. (SS, p. 236; cf. p. 239)

III. Truth and God

Thérèse had a passionate longing for the truth because for her, as we have seen, truth was intimately linked with God. Hence, she admits to Pauline: 'How well I understand Our Lord's words to St. Teresa, our holy Mother: "Do you know, my daughter, who are the ones who really love me? It's those who recognise that everything that can't be referred to me is a lie." Oh, little Mother, I really feel that this is true! Yes, everything outside of God is vanity' (LC, p. 67).[4] Here, Thérèse affirms Teresa's vision that those who really love God are those who know and see all creatures in their relationship to God – as coming constantly and directly from the hands of God who is Truth.

Sin is the great lie because it has no relationship to God and it deceives: it appears as a good, it promises much, but in truth it is futile and destructive, and delivers little. In order to see all things in their relation to God, Thérèse prayed for knowledge of the truth. She affirms: 'I've never acted like Pilate, who refused to listen to the truth. I've always said to God: O my God, I really want to listen to You; I beg You to answer me when I say humbly: What is truth? Make me see things as they really are. Let nothing cause me to be deceived' (LC, p. 105).

IV. Truth and Disordered Attachments

Thérèse is aware of the fact that, because of our disordered attachment to things, there is an unconscious tendency in us to see them through rose-coloured glasses, to project our desires onto things and situations. Here, she is affirming the teaching of John of the Cross – whose writings she knew well and lived fully – that our grasping of things, our disordered desires, and our attachments to creatures, blind us to their true reality and worth. For Thérèse, to know and live the truth is a special grace which allows us to see things clearly for what they are and not to distort their value by over-estimation or an unjust devaluation of them. She once said to Pauline: 'We can say, without any boasting, that we have received very special graces and lights; we stand in the truth and see things in their proper light' (LC, p. 42). Hence, for Thérèse, truth is attained when we see, know and love things as God sees, knows and loves them.

Thérèse is also conscious of the fact that we, as fallen creatures, live in a land of shadows and images; and so we are likely to be deceived, to mistake the shadow and image for the substance. She insists: 'It's only in heaven that we'll see the whole truth about everything. This is impossible on earth' (LC, p. 132). In other words, we can only see the whole truth about creatures when we see them in God, and as God sees them. As such, it is important, as Thérèse was well aware, to refrain from judging – or, at the very least, to be very cautious with regard to our judgments of people and situations.

Pauline recalls: 'Sister Marie of the Sacred Heart told her that when she died the angels would come to her in the company of Our Lord, that she would see them resplendent with light and beauty.' To this, Thérèse had replied: 'All these images do me no good; I can nourish myself on nothing but the truth. This is why I've never wanted any visions. We can't see, here on earth, heaven, the angels, etc., just as they are. I prefer to wait until after my death' (LC, p. 134). Thérèse cannot abide false consolations; she strips things down to their bare reality. She knows all too well – perhaps from her reading of John of the Cross – how visions and other extraordinary experiences are at best ambiguous, and not to be sought or relied upon. As John of the Cross teaches, we can never be certain of the source of such experiences. So, if we seek them or put our trust in them, we can be deceived or live in unreality. Thérèse affirms that only the truth can nourish, satisfy and sustain. In her love and desire for truth, Thérèse fosters a healthy spiritual realism.

V. Truth and the Scriptures

The Scriptures, we have seen, held a special place in the life of Thérèse. She believed that they, in particular, put us in touch with truth: the truth about God and about our life in relationship to God. It is not surprising, then, that Thérèse was especially concerned to learn the truth of the Scriptures. This is why she would have gladly undertaken the laborious task of studying Hebrew and Greek, so as to have access to 'the real text dictated by the Holy Spirit' (LC, p. 132), as she expressed it.

As the Scriptures were a privileged means of contact with the truth, Thérèse desired to guard the integrity of their testimony. She was concerned that those who preach the word of God should not project their own fanciful thoughts onto the sacred texts, but remain with what can honestly be discerned from them. Accordingly, she confesses:

How I would have loved to be a priest in order to preach about the Blessed Virgin! One sermon would be sufficient to say everything I think about this subject.

I'd first make people understand how little is known by us about her life.

We shouldn't say unlikely things or things we don't know anything about! For example, that when she was very little, at the age of three, the Blessed Virgin went up to the Temple to offer herself to God, burning with sentiments of love and extraordinary fervour. While perhaps she went there very simply out of obedience to her parents.

Again, why say, with reference to the aged Simeon's prophetic words, that the Blessed Virgin had the Passion of Jesus constantly before her mind from that moment onward?...

For a sermon on the Blessed Virgin to please me and do me any good, I must see her real life, not her imagined life. (LC, p. 161)

And discussing with Pauline the suggestions of a priest who had said that the Virgin Mary did not experience physical sufferings, Thérèse responds: 'When I was looking at the statue of the Blessed Virgin this evening, I understood this wasn't true. I understood that she suffered not only in soul but also in body. She suffered a lot on her journeys from the cold, the heat, and from fatigue. She fasted very frequently. Yes, she knew what it was to suffer' (LC, p. 158).[5]

VI. Truth and Humility

For Thérèse, truth is inseparable from humility. Humility and truth go together. Humility is living in the truth. So, we cannot be humble without also being truthful. Thérèse applied this principle to her own life, knowing that humility is the simple knowledge of the truth about oneself in relation to God. This is what she says when she begins to write the account of her life in *Story of a Soul*:

> It seems to me that if a little flower could speak, it would tell simply what God has done for it without trying to hide its blessings. It would not say, under the pretext of a false humility, it is not beautiful or without perfume, that the sun has taken away its splendour and the storm has broken its stem when it knows that all this is untrue. The flower about to tell her story rejoices at having to publish the totally gratuitous gifts of Jesus. She knows that nothing in herself was capable of attracting the divine glances, and His mercy alone brought about everything that is good in her. (SS, p. 15)

Pauline records this incident in the infirmary, about eight weeks before Thérèse's death:

> Someone brought her a sheaf of corn; she detached the most beautiful one and said to me:
>
> 'Mother, this ear of corn is the image of my soul: God has entrusted me with graces for myself and for many others.'
>
> Then fearing she had entertained a proud thought, she said:
>
> 'Oh, how I want to be humiliated and mistreated in order to see if I have humility of heart! [that is, to know the truth about herself] However, when I was humbled on former occasions, I was very happy. Yes, it seems to me I am humble. God shows me truth; I feel so much that everything comes from Him.' (LC, pp. 131-2)

A few days later, some nuns started telling her that she was a saint. Thérèse replied: 'No, I'm not a saint;

I've never performed the actions of a saint. I'm a very little soul upon whom God has bestowed graces; that's what I am. What I say is the truth; you'll see this in heaven' (LC, p. 143; cf. p. 131).

Right at the end of her life, just a few hours before she died, Thérèse uttered this rather surprising and bold statement: 'Yes, it seems to me I never sought anything but the truth; yes, I have understood humility of heart... It seems to me I'm humble' (LC, p. 205). This last statement, in which Thérèse affirms her own humility, is problematic for many people. It is natural to be sceptical about anyone who declares his or her own humility. For, almost by definition, one's own humility is not visible to oneself. The truly humble person is unaware of being humble and constantly strives for this virtue. Does this mean, then, that Thérèse's admission of humility is dubious? How can she assert her humility? The answer lies in Thérèse's simple self-confidence in seeking the truth, and identifying humility with truth. She had never consciously avoided the truth, no matter what the cost. So, we may never know if we are humble, but we can tell whether we have consistently and single-mindedly lived and sought the truth. Céline records that Thérèse once said to her: 'To me humility is truth... I do not know whether I am humble, but I do know that I see the truth in all things' (MSST, p. 21).

VII. Truth and Life

Thérèse was careful not to identify living in the truth with having great desires. In Manuscript B, after recounting her immense desires to be ALL for Jesus and to give ALL to Jesus and his Church, Thérèse cries out: 'O my Jesus! I love You! I love the Church, my Mother! I recall that *"the smallest act of* PURE LOVE *is of more value to her than all other works together."*[6] Then she asks Jesus: 'But is PURE LOVE in my heart? Are my measureless desires only but a dream, a folly? Ah! if this be so, Jesus, then enlighten me, for You know I am seeking only the truth' (SS, p. 197).

Here, Thérèse does not simply equate her great desires to give all to Jesus with the actual living out of them. She wants to know if her immense desires reflect, in truth, her actual loving of Jesus. Thérèse is only too aware that while desires are good and necessary, they can also be deceptive – there is often a gap between the desire and the deed. In other words, desires can lull us into a false consciousness, a belief that because the desire exists we also possess the virtue associated with it.

So, when her sister, Marie, reads Manuscript B and becomes despondent because she herself does not have the desire for martyrdom that she thinks would prove her love for Jesus, this is how Thérèse responds to her letter:[7]

My desires of martyrdom *are nothing*;... They are, to tell the truth, the spiritual riches that *render one unjust*, when one rests in them with complacence and when one believes they are *something great*... These desires are a *consolation* that Jesus grants at times to weak souls like mine (and these souls are numerous), but when He does not give this *consolation*, it is a grace of *privilege*. Recall those words of Father [Pichon]: 'The martyrs suffered with joy, and the King of Martyrs suffered with sadness.' Yes, Jesus said: 'Father, let this chalice pass away from me.' Dear Sister, how can you say after this that my desires are the sign of my love? (LT 197)

Thérèse knows that desires themselves do not necessarily indicate the truth of our situation. Underlying this thought is her conviction that the truth is expressed in action and life, not in desires or thoughts: 'The most beautiful thoughts are nothing without good works' (SS, p. 234). This is to say that the truth must be lived out; the truth is known only in the living and doing of it.

Everything Thérèse wrote about, she first lived out. Nothing in her writings is not first tested with her life. So her theology, her spirituality, is experiential. She says, for example: 'Recently, I was writing on charity... and, very often, the nuns came to distract me; then I was very careful not to become impatient, to put into practice what I was writing about' (LC, p. 66). Just a week before her death, Thérèse said to Pauline: 'O Mother, it's very easy to write beautiful things about suffering, but writing is nothing, nothing! One must suffer in order to know!' And she continued: 'I really feel now that what I've said and written is true about everything... It's true that I wanted to suffer much for God's sake, and it's true that I still desire this' (LC, pp. 199-200; cf. p. 205).

VIII. Truth in Thérèse's Spirituality

Truth is at the very heart of Thérèse's life and spirituality of the Little Way, because to speak the truth, and to want to know the truth, is the prerogative of children. As she says in a letter to her aunt: 'Does not truth come out of the mouths of children? Well, you must forgive me if I speak the truth, I who am and want to remain always a child' (LT 178).

Unlike adults, children do not yet know how to be diplomatic in a way that is really deceptive; they do not know how to hide behind words and gestures. There is a certain candour with children; they are guileless, up-front. It is also children who are the most eager to know the truth. They are not satisfied with compromise answers, nor are they fobbed off with facile responses. This is why children are always asking: 'Why? Why? Why?'

Ultimately, for Thérèse, truth is Jesus. So, to the extent that we live in Jesus, we live in the truth and we know the truth. In a letter to Céline, Thérèse quotes from the Gospel of John (Jn 14:23), and gives this commentary:

'If anyone *loves* me, he *will keep* my *word*, and my Father *will love* him, and *we* will come to him, and *we* will make in him *our* abode.' To keep the *word* of Jesus, that is the sole condition of our happiness, the proof of our love for Him. But what, then, is this word?... It seems to me that the *word* of Jesus is *Himself*... He, *Jesus*, the *Word*, the *Word* of *God*! He tells us further on in the same gospel of St. John, praying to his Father for His disciples, He expresses Himself thus: 'Sanctify them by your *word*, your word is *truth*.' In another place, Jesus teaches us that He is the way, the *truth*, the life. We know, then, what is the *Word* that we must keep; like Pilate, we shall not ask Jesus: 'What is *Truth*?' We possess *Truth*. We *are keeping* Jesus in our *hearts*! (LT 165)

EPILOGUE

On October 19, 1997, John Paul II declared Thérèse a 'Doctor of the Church'.[1] This title is bestowed posthumously on a person known for: eminent learning, great holiness, and writings which have benefited the whole Church.

Not everyone in the Church, though, acclaimed the doctorate of Thérèse. In fact, it caused surprise and consternation among many – especially among academics, and those with formal qualifications in theology. No one contested Thérèse's holiness, or the beneficial influence of her doctrine in the Church. Rather, the question mark was about the criterion of 'eminent learning'.

It is, of course, debatable as to whether *any* of the saints declared 'Doctors of the Church' would meet these three criteria if they were strictly applied. Although many Fathers of the Church, for example, would undoubtedly qualify as holy and learned, it is questionable as to how influential or beneficial their writings have been in the lives of the Christian faithful. We also need to ask how 'eminent learning' is to be defined. Is it confined to philosophical language in analysing the mysteries of the faith? No – for there is also a type of learning that is not 'academic' or intellectual as such, but intensely personal and profound, and described as 'mystical theology'. God can teach and reveal himself in a truly deep and personal way to 'little ones', those without any *formal* theological learning (cf. Mt 11:25-27; 1Cor 1:17ff.). Speaking of herself at the age of 14, Thérèse attributes to God whatever knowledge and wisdom she has acquired of divine things. She writes:

Jesus showered His graces so lavishly upon His little flower, He, who cried out in His mortal life: '*I thank thee, Father, that thou hast hidden these things from the wise and the prudent and revealed them to babes*', willed to have His mercy shine out in me. Because I was little and weak He lowered Himself to me, and He instructed me secretly in the *things* of His *love*. Ah! had the learned who spent their life in study come to me, undoubtedly they would have been astonished to see a child of fourteen understand perfection's secrets, secrets all their knowledge cannot reveal because to possess them one has to be poor in spirit! (SS, p. 105)

Thérèse was certainly not an academic or an intellectual in the generally accepted sense, even though she would have liked to steep herself in sacred learning. She possessed no formal qualifications and would almost certainly have baulked at the idea of being declared a 'Doctor'! Nevertheless, like Jesus himself, Thérèse reminds us that the things of God are not to be plundered by human ingenuity and strength. On the contrary, human cleverness may be an obstacle to attaining the things of God. These things of God are the fruits of grace, the unmerited gifts to those who, recognising their poverty, are ready to receive them humbly from God. And to receive them, to be truly poor in spirit, Thérèse teaches us that we must become like little children. Indeed, this is what Jesus meant when he said: 'I tell you solemnly, unless you change and become like little children you will never enter the kingdom of heaven' (Mt 18:3).

We have seen that the writings of Thérèse did not originate from her own personal initiative, but from the requests of others. For most of her life, Thérèse had no pretensions of being a teacher, or of having any special doctrine to impart to others. It was only towards the end of her life that she had an intuition that her writings should be preserved and made known; that they would be of some spiritual benefit to others – to 'little souls' like herself.

Thérèse's main concern was not with writing treatises, but with living, as generously as she could, the hidden, silent and humble life of love of a faithful Carmelite. Her constant ambition was to love Jesus as he had never been loved before, and to attain to holiness. It was this desire and ambition that consumed her and led her to develop her Little Way. Thérèse's spirituality, then, was born in the crucible of a personal struggle to give herself to God. This struggle involved coming to accept, ever more deeply and humbly, her own limitations (those of any creature): the 'littleness' of weakness, poverty, inadequacy; and at the same time it entailed growing in her unwavering confidence in God's merciful love.

In an age rife with Jansenism and its emphasis on a God of exacting justice, Thérèse's spirituality, her 'little way' to holiness, was firmly grounded in the Scriptures and especially the Gospels. The word of God was Thérèse's ultimate teacher and guide on her spiritual journey. It was *the* viewpoint that guided and shaped her life and discipleship. Through the Scriptures she also arrived at a God of loving mercy without compromising God's justice. This evangelical understanding of God enabled Thérèse not to become discouraged by her 'littleness', but to persevere in spite of it – and ultimately because of it.

Holiness is the fundamental vocation of all the baptised. As such, it is not reserved to a spiritual elite, but is the common Christian vocation. It is the goal of every true disciple of Jesus. However, in the daily grind of our lives with its many demands, we can find this goal remote and unattainable. Our efforts to strive towards it often seem fruitless. We discover that we are not made of the stuff of saints! So we feel that there is an unbridgeable chasm between our good desires and our inability to live them. Like Thérèse, we can be burdened with unrealistic notions of what constitutes true holiness, and so become discouraged. Unlike Thérèse, however, we may become content to settle for mediocrity in our discipleship, convinced that holiness is not for us – an unrealisable dream!

From her own personal and often humiliating struggle to give herself wholly to God, Thérèse fashioned a way of holiness for 'little souls' – people who feel themselves weak and powerless, but who nonetheless aspire to intimate communion with God. She leads us to him by the ordinary and the mundane, and encourages us to journey to God with the invincible weapons of love and confidence. She teaches us how our everyday humdrum life, with its sufferings and joys, is the place where we are given the possibility of drawing near to God. In short, Thérèse teaches us how to ascend to the heights of communion with God, while remaining on the plains of our everyday life.

It is my hope that this exploration of Thérèse's spirituality will remove any false notions of holiness.

I believe that Thérèse shows us a way of attaining to holiness that is not intimidating. It asks of us no spiritual heroics and makes no *unrealisable* demands. Nevertheless, it would be untrue to say that it makes no demands. On the contrary, it asks of us everything – 'to give ALL to Jesus'. This 'giving all', however, is not about 'growing up' in the sense of becoming independent and self-sufficient but, paradoxically, it is all about 'growing down', becoming truly a little child who is utterly dependent on God and confident of his help.

NOTES

Prologue

1. Hans Urs von Balthasar, *Two Sisters in the Spirit: Thérèse of Lisieux & Elizabeth of the Trinity*, San Francisco: Ignatius Press, 1992.

2. Conrad De Meester, OCD, *With Empty Hands: The Message of Thérèse of Lisieux*, Homebush, NSW: St Paul Publications, 1982. This book has since been published in a revised edition by Burns & Oates (London & New York, 2002). It is the essence of De Meester's much longer work: *The Power of Confidence: Genesis and Structure of the 'Way of Spiritual Childhood' of Saint Thérèse of Lisieux*, New York: Alba House, 1998 (first published in French in 1969).

3. François Jamart, OCD, *Complete Spiritual Doctrine of St. Thérèse of Lisieux*, New York: Alba House, 1961.

Chapter One

1. Thérèse says on this subject: 'I had only Marie, and she was indispensable to me, so to speak. I told my scruples only to her and was so obedient that my confessor never knew my ugly malady' (SS, p. 88).

2. Addressing Mother Marie, Thérèse says: 'I remember when I was still a postulant that I had such violent temptations to satisfy myself and to find a few crumbs of pleasure that I was obliged to walk rapidly by your door and to cling firmly to the banister of the staircase in order not to turn back. There came into my mind a crowd of permissions to seek; in a word, dear Mother, I found a thousand reasons for pleasing my nature' (SS, p. 237; cf. p. 223).

Chapter Two

1. The more minor writings of Thérèse, such as her *Poems* and *Plays*, are not explored.
2. Adolphe Roulland was a missionary priest working in China. Maurice Bellière was a seminarian who joined the White Fathers, training to be a missionary for Africa.

Chapter Three

1. In John Paul II, *Divini Amoris Scientia* (*The Science of Divine Love*), his Apostolic Letter proclaiming Thérèse a Doctor of the Universal Church, October 19, 1997, #9.
2. Exodus, Leviticus, Deuteronomy, 2 Samuel, 1 Kings, 2 Kings, Tobias, Psalms, Proverbs, Ecclesiastes, Song of Songs, Wisdom, Isaiah and Ezekiel.
3. Romans, 1 Corinthians, 2 Corinthians, Galatians, Philippians, Titus and Revelation.
4. Thomas à Kempis, *The Imitation of Christ*, London: Burns & Oates, 1959, p. 23.
5. Céline writes: 'For her hours of meditation, Thérèse leaned heavily on the Gospels and, in a lesser degree, on certain books of the Old Testament.' And we read this note: 'At that period, young religious were not always permitted to read all the books of the Old Testament.' Céline continues: 'This was especially true of the latter part of her life when no other book, even among those books which had helped her in previous years, succeeded in enkindling her devotion' (MSST, p. 105).
6. Thérèse had this deep conviction with regard to her desires. She once said: '[The Lord] has always given me what I desire or rather He has made me desire what He wants to give me' (SS, p. 250).

Chapter Four

1. Thérèse writes 'ALL', not only three times in capital letters, but she also underlines it two, three and five times respectively.
2. In *Story of a Soul*, Thérèse recalls an incident from her childhood which she sees as reflecting her whole response to life – and especially to her relationship with God. This incident is as

follows: 'One day, Léonie, thinking she was too big to be playing any longer with dolls, came to us [Céline and Thérèse] with a basket filled with dresses and pretty pieces for making others; her doll was resting on top. "Here, my little sisters, *choose*; I'm giving you all this." Céline stretched out her hand and took a little ball of wool that pleased her. After a moment's reflection, I stretched out mine saying: 'I choose all!' and I took the basket without further ceremony... This little incident of my childhood is a summary of my whole life; later on when perfection was set before me, I understood that to become *a saint* one had to suffer much, seek out always the most perfect thing to do, and forget self. I understood, too, there were many degrees of perfection and each soul was free to respond to the advances of Our Lord, to do little or much for Him, in a word, to *choose* among the sacrifices He was asking. Then, as in the days of my childhood, I cried out: "My God, '*I choose all!*' I don't want to be a *saint by halves*, I'm not afraid to suffer for You, I fear only one thing: to keep my *own will*; so take it, for '*I choose all*' that You will!'" (SS, p. 27).

3. As a young religious, Thérèse wore 'a small penitential cross. Its sharp iron points entered her flesh and she fell ill. "Such a trifle would not have caused this," she said, "if God had not wished to make me understand that the great austerities of the saints are not meant for me or for the little souls who are to walk by the same path of spiritual childhood."... Later it was Mother Agnes who disclosed to the ecclesiastical authorities Thérèse's long-considered and proved method of using the unplanned and undesigned mortifications of life as a means of sanctity. "She had no use for mortifications that preoccupied her and hindered her from cleaving to God. She told me that warm-hearted but imprudent souls were often deceived by the devil who drove them to excesses which damaged their health and prevented them from fulfilling their duties... she confessed that at the start of her life in the convent she thought she was doing well and imitating the saints by practising tricks to make her food insipid. 'But,' she added, 'I put all that kind of behaviour behind me a long time ago. Now when the food is to my taste, I am grateful to God. When it is not, I accept it as a mortification. Such mortification, which has not been sought for, seems to me

to be the safest and most sanctifying.'"": see John Beevers, *Storm of Glory: St. Thérèse of Lisieux*, London: Sheed & Ward, 1949, pp. 107-8; cf. SS, p. 143.

4. With regard to the role of 'desires' as inspired by God, see SS, pp. 152, 175, 207, 250 & 276.

5. See von Balthasar, *op. cit.*, p. 298.

6. As we have seen, Thérèse did not dismiss or criticise other ways of journeying to God, such as those travelled by the 'great' saints.

7. My italics in this and the previous quotation.

8. In Jamart, *op. cit.*, p. 54; cf. SS, p. 165.

Chapter Five

1. John Clarke, OCD, translator of *Story of a Soul*, in his Prologue to that work: see SS, pp. 4-5.

2. See this beautiful description of Thérèse's favourite day of the week, Sunday, a scene of family warmth into which prayer was smoothly woven: 'What shall I say of the winter evenings at home, especially the Sunday evenings? Ah! how I loved, after the *game of checkers* was over, to sit with Céline on Papa's knees. He used to sing, in his beautiful voice, airs that filled the soul with profound thoughts, or else, rocking us gently, he recited poems that taught the eternal truths. Then we all went upstairs to say our night prayers together and the little Queen was alone near her King, having only to look at him to see how the saints pray' (SS, p. 43).

3. Thérèse says: 'everything pointed to the fact that he would die impenitent' (SS, p. 99). But she found her prayer answered, when she read in the paper that as Pranzini was about to be executed, he grabbed the priest's crucifix and kissed it. She calls Pranzini 'my "*first child*"' (SS, p. 100). Thérèse also says: 'this sign was a perfect replica of the grace Jesus had given me when He attracted me to pray for sinners' (SS, p. 100) – the reason being that Pranzini had kissed the crucifix, and it was before a picture of Jesus on the Cross that Thérèse had felt called to pray for '*great sinners*' (SS, p. 99).

4. To illustrate this idea, Thérèse uses the image of a torrent of water which drags everything in its path along with it: 'Just as

a torrent, throwing itself with impetuosity into the ocean, drags after it everything it encounters in its passage, in the same way, O Jesus, the soul who plunges into the shoreless ocean of Your Love, draws with her all the treasures she possesses.' And she spells out what these treasures are: 'Lord, You know it, I have no other treasures than the souls it has pleased You to unite to mine' (SS, p. 254).

5. See also these two important passages in other letters to Pauline, written around the same time: 'I don't understand the retreat I am making; I think of nothing, in a word, I am in a very dark subterranean passage!... Oh! ask Jesus, you who are my light, that He not permit souls to be deprived of lights that they need because of me, but that my darkness serve to enlighten them... Ask Him, too, that I make a good retreat and that He may be as pleased as He can be; then I, too, will be pleased, and I will consent, if this be His will, to walk all my life on the dark road on which I am, provided that one day I reach the summit of the mountain of Love. But I believe this will not be here below' (LT 112). And: 'My soul is always in the subterranean passage, but it is *very happy*, yes, happy to have no consolation whatsoever, for I find that then its love is not like the love of earthly fiancées who are always looking at the hands of their fiancés to see if they have brought them any gifts, or else at their faces to catch there a smile of love which delights them' (LT 115).

6. My italics.

Chapter Six

1. This theme of 'singing the mercies of the Lord' recurs often in *Story of a Soul*: see SS, pp. 205, 208, 245 & 248.

2. Cf. 'This is the mystery of my vocation, my whole life, and especially the mystery of the privileges Jesus showered on my soul' (SS, p. 13).

3. See Chapter Four.

4. See also Thérèse's 'Act of Oblation to Merciful Love', where she writes: 'In order to live in one single act of perfect Love, I OFFER MYSELF AS A VICTIM OF HOLOCAUST TO YOUR MERCIFUL LOVE, asking You to consume me incessantly, allowing the waves of *infinite tenderness* shut up within You to

overflow into my soul, and that thus I may become a *martyr* of Your *Love*, O my God!' (SS, p. 277).

5. Note, too, the words 'in one instant'; they recall Thérèse's 'Christmas grace': 'God would have to work a little miracle to make me *grow up* in an instant, and this miracle He performed on that unforgettable Christmas day... On that *night of light* began the third period of my life, the most beautiful and the most filled with graces from heaven. The work I had been unable to do in ten years was done by Jesus in one instant, contenting himself with my *good will* which was never lacking' (SS, pp. 97-8).

6. This raises the issue of grace and free will, which is why, I believe, Thérèse uses the words 'so to speak'.

7. She writes: 'Perfection consists in doing His will, in being what He wills us to be' (SS, p. 14).

8. John Paul II said these words during a visit to Lisieux in 1980: 'Of St Thérèse of Lisieux it can be said with conviction that God chose her to reveal directly to the men and women of our time the central reality of the Gospel, that God is our Father and we are his children. This is the unique genius of St Thérèse of Lisieux. Thanks to her the entire Church has found once again the whole simplicity and freshness of the gospel truth, which has its origin and source in the heart of Christ himself.'

Chapter Seven

1. In William L Shirer, *Gandhi: A Memoir*, London: Sphere Books, 1981, pp. 111 & 240.

2. Edith Stein, *Self-Portrait in Letters 1916-1942*, Washington, DC: ICS Publications, 1993, Letter 259, p. 272.

3. When Thérèse was a very young child, Zélie wrote, in another letter to Pauline: '[Thérèse] wouldn't tell a lie for all the gold in the world and she has a spirit about her that I have not seen in any of you' (SS, p. 28). Then, when she became very ill at the age of ten, Thérèse was afflicted with scruples, worrying if she had only pretended to be ill (cf. SS, p. 62).

4. Thérèse is quoting here from Teresa of Avila's *Life* 40:1.

5. See also Thérèse's rejection of ancient stories about the Child Jesus performing what she aptly called 'useless miracles' – such

as breathing life into birds of clay. 'No,' she comments, about the Holy Family, 'everything in their life was done just as in our own' (LC, p. 159).

6. A quotation from John of the Cross, *The Spiritual Canticle* 29:2.

7. See Marie's letter to Thérèse, in GC II, p. 997.

Epilogue

1. See his Apostolic Letter, *Divini Amoris Scientia* (*The Science of Divine Love*), *op. cit.*

MOUNT CARMEL
A Review of the Spiritual Life

UPON THIS MOUNTAIN: PRAYER IN THE CARMELITE TRADITION

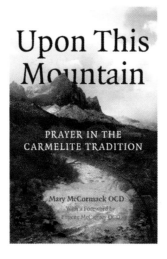

Mary McCormack OCD

Teresian Press

◆►══◎ ◎══◄◆

Available from:

**Carmelite Book Service
Boars Hill
Oxford OX1 5HB**

www.carmelitebooks.com

Price £4.00

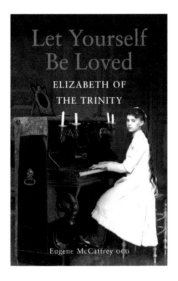

Some Forthcoming Titles from the Teresian Press

A Moment of Prayer – A Life of Prayer
  – Conrad De Meester, OCD

What Carmel Means to Me
  – Edited by James McCaffrey, OCD
  & Joanne Mosley

John of the Cross: Seasons of Prayer
  – Iain Matthew, OCD

How Do I Pray Today?
  – Edited by James McCaffrey, OCD
  & Joanne Mosley

Elizabeth of the Trinity
  – Joanne Mosley